About the Author

Gordon MacLellan is a Manchester-based environmental artsworker, working with communities to create celebrations of the relationships between people and places. After training as a zoologist and then as a teacher, he taught in Malawi, returning to Britain after a few years to work in environmental education. He combines his scientific background with a rich vein of creativity as a dancer, storyteller and mask-maker. While he teaches and lectures on shamanism, Gordon finds that this earth-centred spirituality also inspires all aspects of his everyday work.

Shamanism

Piatkus Guides

A PIATKUS GUIDE

Shamanism

Gordon MacLellan

PIATKUS

To all my relatives

First published in 1999 by
Judy Piatkus (Publishers) Ltd
5 Windmill Street, London W1P 1HF
www.piatkus.co.uk

A catalogue record for this book is available from the British Library

ISBN 0-7499-2023-8

Typeset by Action Publishing Technology Limited, Gloucester
Printed and bound in Great Britain by
Mackays of Chatham PLC

Contents

Acknowledgements

Thanks to Jo Crow and all the Mad Shamans for endless provocation and inspiration.

Introduction

Shamanism is an ancient spiritual path that explores a way of living in harmony with the world around us. It is possibly the oldest kind of organised spiritual expression. No-one knows how it really began, whether it evolved as a set of ideas in scattered cultures across the globe, or whether a core of early humans carried its first forms with them on epic migrations. But the essential ideas of a living, spirit-filled world and pathfinders who speak to the spirits are found all over the planet.

Shamanism has been practised in various forms all over the world for thousands of years, growing with communities into more complicated faiths and absorbing or being absorbed by new religious movements. The common features lie in the underlying concept of a living, conscious world and in the principles that inspire the practice of shamanism, although each unique form uses a different variety of tools and techniques.

Shamans perceive a world where everything is alive, where spirit — that sense of self and personality that we find in ourselves — can be found to some measure in every other inhabitant of the world. In a shamanic culture that awareness may be shared by everyone, but the expert in communication between humans and the non-human world is the shaman. Shamans serve their community by finding the paths to harmony for their people that will also contribute to the growth and survival of the whole world. They will not benefit their people at the expense of everything else.

A shamanic harmony is not a passive state but an active, dynamic relationship with the living world that recognises the relationships that lie between all that exists. The shaman's peace is a vibrant, thrilling pattern of connections where life and growth are celebrated and where the world itself is a waking part of the equation, bringing the percep- tions of animal, plant, stone and water to the shaman's deliberations.

To a shaman, the spirits of other living things are independ- ent beings in their own right, with their own agendas, their own quarrels, hopes and fears. The shaman has to be able to meet and talk to those beings to convince them to cooperate with the community. By learning long-established techniques involving song, music, dance, drugs, pain or stillness, shamans learn to separate themselves from everyday reality. By going into a trance they can enter realms where they can communi- cate directly with the spirits. There they can develop relationships with spirit helpers and draw upon initiation cere- monies (acceptance by the spirits), Vigil and Visionquest (recognition of their abilities as a shaman by the whole world), conduct healing and find those safe paths to peace with the world that they seek for both individuals and the community as a whole.

There is no single philosophy or set of teachings that defines the practice of shamanism. It evolved in many cultures over the world as a tool for survival. Its forms are diverse and unpredictable. Being a shaman is more about following a vocation and fulfilling a role than pursuing any particular faith.

Throughout this book I draw upon my experiences and those of modern and traditional shamanic friends to support my ideas and explain the diversity of shamanic practices. I have tried to unearth the personal qualities and experiences that you will need to understand what might go to make a shaman. You might disagree with what follows, it might prove pointless and meaningless to you, or perhaps it will be just what you are looking for.

My Story

I first became interested in shamanism as a child, when I watched a toad opening its eyes; a lump of brown and green transforming, wet mud animating. That moment has stayed with me ever since, and while I pottered around my child-hood doing other things, the spirit of the toad was always there.

One day I realised that Toad had been with me since that first encounter, creeping her quiet way deep into the heart of me. We have been like that for years now, friends, compan-ions, a shaman and a spirit, exploring people, this world and the spirit worlds together – getting lost, making mistakes and stumbling through alarms, wonders and strange delights.

I am a 'patterner' – I work with groups of people to explore and express their own relationships with the world. I help people create celebrations and in the process they might discover something of themselves and something of their own connections to the world around them.

For me, this is a shamanic process: it is inspired by the world I live in and its purpose is to help people explore those relationships for themselves. The spirits are there for me, even if they are not always there for the people I work with, and while some people call me a shaman, to others I am 'that mad guy who gets us to do crazy things'. My career and spirituality are all tied up together, the whole being a celebration of life in a living world.

Shamanism and You

I hope to offer ways for you, living in a Western, technological society, divorced from any shamanism your ancestors might have practised, to make new connections and find new ways of living with the earth.

Shamanism will help you pick a path through the trials of life to find a way of harmony with the world. While the ancient techniques may not always seem relevant to modern life-styles, the underlying principles that inspired those techniques and the qualities a shaman needs to develop are as relevant now as they ever were. It is easy to despair when we live in a world of concrete and tower blocks, a world hammered by pollution, ozone depletion and exploitation of the earth's resources. As a shaman you can find the promise of new life and the ancient disciplines of shamanism can help you to find paths that lead to healing, communication with the spirits of the living world and a personal path to a life that moves in harmony with the world.

A Few Practical Points

Traditional and modern

I distinguish between 'traditional' and 'modern' shamanism, not to make any point about the validity of either source but for convenience of writing and reading. 'Traditional' shamanism is seen as those practices that belong to an inherited, unbroken, often ancient lineage within a society, and are a part of the essential structure of that society. 'Modern' shamanism describes the new forms evolving in technological societies in which the ancestral sources are long gone or grown too tenuous really to describe a surviving form. No relative value is attached to these labels.

Vocabulary and gender

I avoid words such as shamanka, neo-shamanism (you are either a shaman or you are not – the spirits do not call you a neo-anything, or would this make them neo-spirits?), shamanising, shamanness and shamanry as awkward and unnecessary. Shamans may be male, female or express their own gender variant, so, to keep you on your toes, personal pronouns vary from chapter to chapter. With generic words such as 'god', I have used this form throughout rather than the more cumbersome 'god/dess' or 'god or goddess'. In doing so I am including deities of whatever gender and no male prerogative is intended.

1

Old People, New People

The Beginning

Over time, our distant ancestors realised that the world they lived in was more than just a place to eat, sleep, breed and die. They learned that their world was as alive as they themselves were, and that their survival was bound up with more than the need to keep warm and have enough to eat. They knew that just as the world affected them through physical things – rain, sun, the changing seasons, the migration of animals – it also reached out to them in other ways; maybe they heard the voices of their prey speaking out of the night and the dreams of the hills in the silence of the painted caves.

Our ancestors' world was alive, and they were as deeply woven into the fabric of it, the living and dying of it, as any of the plants they gathered or the animals they hunted. The world spoke to them and they learned to listen, to enter the conversation, to find the paths of least disturbance through this great interwoven web of life – the trails that allowed the tribe to survive and even to thrive without outgrowing the supplies its environment provided.

The pattern ran deeper than simple, or even subtle, resource management, for the people were as intrinsically a part of that world as any element of the landscape. With the awareness of that connection came the discovery of kinship and bonds between animal, plant, landscape and people, and a sense of responsibility, obligations of protection and cere-monies of empowerment. These relationships needed to be worked on, explored, developed and protected. This was not a world that belonged to a humanity with exclusive claims to its use. It was a world of independent, interdependent and diverse intelligences, and the responsibilities of finding ways of living together, of recognising lives taken and lives given, and the sun and rain that bring the world to life and burn it or drown it into death again, belonged to the community. It was a world of animism: of consciousness, of life, of spirit perme-ating everything.

Among these communities on the edge of survival, the shaman evolved as one component of a tribe's survival skills. Alongside those who gathered and those who hunted, fished or tanned hide, were those who found the safe paths through the world, the ways of living that kept the tribe at peace with its non-human neighbours. Recognising that all life is about dying, the shaman's job was not to avoid or disguise killing, but to explain it, justify it, offer respect for lives taken by the tribe, lives given by the world, and to bring to her people the thoughts of the spirit world on their conduct and the path they followed. The shaman was the pathfinder for her people, picking a route through the interwoven trails of all the other inhabitants of the world, both human and non-human. They have been with us ever since.

The Present

Today shamanic ideas and techniques lie hidden in many modern spiritual traditions, and often descriptions of shamanic practices may remind you of things you have ex perienced. But the shamans themselves are still with us, and far from being decrepit with age or crippled by its antiquity, shamanism is tough, vibrant and surviving. While some tradi- tional shamanic cultures are reeling from the impact of modern Western technological society, others are holding their own, proving to be resilient and accommodating. Roman Catholic saints are invoked alongside older gods and demons by Central American healers; African masked dancers dance their ancestors, their animals and the spirits of motor cars and aeroplanes. New spirits evolve in traditional cultures as their shamans encounter the forces of technology – guns and water pumps. Such new spirits are incorporated into traditional ways of working. Modern shamans in Western cities are meeting other spirits, people growing out of dense cities and high-rise office blocks, stilt-legged, stalk- ing spirits who step out along lamp-lit streets in the early hours of the morning.

It is very easy for a society cushioned in technological comfort and far from that apparent 'edge of survival' to be dismissive of 'magical' interpretations of the natural world. We feel safe in labelling an animistic worldview as 'primi- tive' or 'superstitious' and forget that such cultures generally have a much longer and less destructive track record than our own. Should the success of a culture be measured by the numbers of its people, the expansion of its territories, its consumption of resources or its endurance? These were, and still are, people whose understanding of the world is unsur- passed in its subtlety and precision. And even if all this talk of spirits and communication with the spirit world is just a story to back up generations of accumulated experience, it could still teach us ways of living within our resources and achieving some form of sustainable relationship with our planet.

At last, while we have thought ourselves safe from the vagaries of the world, we are beginning to realise that we are back on the edge of survival. The 'edge' may have changed from immediate starvation or the cold of winter to collapsing fish stocks, a thinning ozone layer and the unforeseen consequences of pollution, but the outcome remains the same: our global tribe is again living on that edge. At last, we recognise the need to review our relationship with the natural world, that we are not masters and the earth an endless larder for our plundering. We are beginning to realise again that we are as much a part of its dynamic processes as everything else and that we need to find ways of moving safely within those processes.

This does not necessarily mean spiritual processes, but for many people the depth and subtlety of our relationship with the world moves from analysis and calculation into the realms of emotion, intuition and inspiration. Established religions are reviewing their teachings about our relationship with the world, and concepts of 'stewardship' are replacing 'ownership' and the glory of creation as an expression of Divine Will celebrated. In the West, other beliefs are also returning, or new forms growing, with the revival of the 'nature' religions, attracting people interested in exploring active, personal connections to a living world where the Divine can be found as much in the physical world as in some distant celestial realm. The old gods of nature, sometimes wearing new faces, are returning, celebrated in new ways and old through the changing year and the wonders of a living world. And when people turn to animism they find the spirits are still there, too.

A community's guide to relationships with the spirits might be referred to as a 'pathfinder', 'healer', 'holy man' or 'walker between the worlds'. The term 'shaman' comes from the Tungus people of Siberia and means 'ecstatic one', describing a visionary who travelled to the spirit world on behalf of his people. Purists argue that this term should still only be applied to that role among those people, but it has now moved into wider currency and is well established as a description of 'a person who works with spirits'. All is open to wide interpretations, but in *Shamanism* I will try to slip behind the wide variety of terms and find the essential attitudes and practices that go to make a shaman. There is no overall set of rules that define a shaman, but the underlying similarities in the role of these pathfinders, why they do it and how they do it, can be explored. In the heart of it all are concepts of *community*, *trance* and *ecstasy*.

Community

Shamans serve the communities they belong to. They are bound up in the relationship of people, land and spirit, often to their own cost. Traditional shamanism can be a chosen path, a willing vocation, or an obligation thrust upon someone. The demands upon its practitioners are often exacting, sometimes painful, and rarely a route to instant health, wealth and happiness. It is the role that they fill that identifies a person as a shaman. You become a shaman, not when you pass an exam or qualify for a certificate but when you are recognised as such by your community. That is as true now as it has ever been: you may do the workshops, buy the labels, kit yourself out with drum, rattle and feathers, but it is only when you work with people, land and spirit that you become a shaman.

In traditional societies the relationship between shaman and community is clear, the dynamics having evolved over the centuries. People know how to relate to their shamans, how to support them, pay them, and even get rid of them as occasion demands. For modern shamans, however, our communities are harder to define – is it the people who live in your street? You colleagues at work? Your friends? Members of your coven, lodge or church? Or whoever needs you at the time? The community you serve might be all those groups at one time or another. We do not, however, generally live in a society that recognises shamans or appreciates their work, and while people may use you as a shaman, they may not identify the role in shamanic terms. They turn to you because you can help, through listening, laughing, making them dance, creating ceremonies, helping them to be still, bringing them to a new relationship with their world, but you may never be called a shaman.

A modern shaman has to find new paths through life. Traditional skills may inform you and teachings inspire you, but you have to find ways that the communities you work with now will respond to. Much of this book will explore ways of building new bridges between the worlds, of doing a shamanic job in a non-shamanic society.

Trance and Ecstasy

A shaman needs to be able to enter the spirit world and work with those spirits as an active participant. Shamans are rarely passive mediums or a channel for spirit voices. A shaman is expected to enter a dialogue, sometimes even a downright squabble with the spirits she meets. To do this, she has to be able to set her own spirit free, if not from her body, then at least from the distractions of everyday life. The period of separation from the mundane run of things is known as trance. Trance is an ecstatic state. It may be entered through stillness and silence or by singing, drumming or dancing. Trance for a shaman is a state of heightened spiritual awareness, allowing her to perceive beings and forces that are not registered by our usual senses. The period of detachment might be very gentle and shallow, so allowing the shaman to talk to her clients even while listening to the spirits, or it can reach deeper, where she seems 'dead to the world' or where the spirits share her body and she drums or performs wild, whirling dances with the spirits looking out of her eyes and rejoicing in the beat of feet on the floor and the rhythm in the blood.

A shaman's work is often hard and unpleasant – helping the dead find their way home, wrestling health back from a spirit of illness or 'dis-ease' – but even in the hardest of work, shamans may still feel the sense of wonder, release and glory that is the passion of the spirit world.

Performance or Sham?

In their public work, shamans are often spectacular, using singing, music, dancing, dramatic ceremonies, drugs, blood-letting and sleight of hand to draw people into the enchantment of the experience. Shamans have been condemned as charlatans, tricking their audiences with amateur dramatics and fooling them into some level of subservience. However, such critics might well be approaching a shaman's work from an essentially Western Christian expectation of spiritual experience as restrained or at least dignified. The participants at a shamanic ceremony need to be assured that something is happening; dance, song and music allow them to follow and support their shaman's work, while drugs might even allow them to share the experience itself. Any exponent of street theatre can describe the power of performance to draw an audience into the passion of a situation and to inspire a willing suspension of disbelief. Traditional shamanism may not meet our expectations of what a spiritual or religious experience should be, yet it should not be judged against our standards but by the survival of the shaman among her people. If she cannot 'come up with the goods', sooner or later she will lose those that turn to her for help, and even her whole community, as they look elsewhere for their healing and guidance. She will quite possibly lose her life, too. Failed shamans are not known for their longevity.

Who Becomes a Shaman?

There are no absolutes in shamanism; no single 'this is the way to do it', no definite 'shamanic way'. Shamanism is a personal calling. Even when working within a long-established tradition, individual shamans will do things their own way. Teachers may help apprentices perfect techniques and listen to or interpret Visions, but those apprentices still have to forge their own relationships with the spirit world and find the power to act for themselves.

The boundaries and expected skills of a shaman vary from society to society. A shaman may be male or female, heterosexual, homosexual or bisexual or express other gender variants where those terms have any meaning at all. They may be young or old. In some cultures people become shamans as their children grow older and independent, in others, the Vision that indentifies the shaman may come at any age. A shaman may also work all her life with the spirits or find that those abilities leave her after time.

As a community's 'pathfinder', shamans may be healers of the sick, guides for the dead, channels through which the ancestors may speak, guardians of tradition and the heart of resistance to change. Shamans may also be tricksters, fools, clowns and 'contraries' – people who challenge us by throwing convention back in our faces, making us question what is 'right and proper' by being everything we think people should not be. Shamans 'break reality': when healing you, a shaman may choose to shock you out of your complacency; when guiding her people a shaman may do everything the wrong way round, upsetting people, throwing them off-balance, making them find their own feet and laughing at their own self-righteousness. Shamans protect our paths through life; in traditional societies that often means protecting old customs for those are the paths that have guaranteed survival over the generations, but they must also be sensitive to the changing world and find new paths as situations change. In a modern Western society, where we may have forgotten or lost our trails through the world, shamans need to start afresh, picking new paths out of the confusion of our lives.

Shamans are often uncomfortable people to be around. They may be there to serve their people but they also serve the spirits they work with. Shamans protect the patterns of the living world, the Web of life (see Chapter 2). One way of looking at a shaman's work is to see it as a way of protecting patterns, making sure those trails stay open and accessible, charting their changes and finding ways of bringing us back into the greater pattern rather than existing on a private, human highway through the life of the planet. When a shaman heals, she is simply helping you step back on to your personal path; when she provokes her people she is shaking them up enough to, hopefully, find a new path out of their current traffic jam.

As well as serving their people shamans serve the world, and that is where the passion lies. Descriptions of the Visions that bring a shaman into power are often full of the numinous. Through hardship and isolation, the shaman steps out of the everyday world and into a world of wonder, a sense of a glorious whole that never quite leaves her. That awareness of something Other is always there in the shaman, a wondering passion that inspires and empowers her. Shamans are the pathfinders, workers with trance and ecstasy.

Activities and Meditations

Each chapter in this book includes exercises to help you explore the concepts discussed. These activities and meditations will help you experience a shaman's world, taking the first steps on the path to becoming a shaman yourself. You should start by practising the exercises in the order in which they are presented. After that, however, you will have to decide for yourself what pattern your activities should take: early experiences will show you areas you will need to return to several times and the spirits themselves will have their own advice to offer as to where your training should lead.

Shamanic training often feels rather unpredictable: it seems to work in spirals rather than straightforward lines of learning. A shamanic training never ends – even when you have been working for many years, you will still find yourself coming back to the early exercises presented here. We never stop needing to 'touch stillness' or to practise our 'visualisation'.

Beginnings and Groundings

It is helpful if each exercise is formally opened and closed. Actions that mark the beginning of an activity session help your mind – and later your spirit family – prepare for the work ahead, separating this time from your everyday life. At the end of a session a 'closing' or 'grounding' activity enables you to step firmly and clearly out of that magical space and back into your everyday life.

An offering

It is useful to open a session, even if it is only a short personal meditation, with an offering to the spirits – a gift given to a friend. The act of offering provides an initial focus, a starting point for your concentration and an opportunity for you to be clear about what you are going to do and why. A single candle lit with intention and reverence becomes a prayer to the world with the flickering purity of its flame.

Smoke is widespread as a traditional carrier of prayers. You might fume grains of incense on a charcoal block, burn herbs in fire or smoulder herbs in a ball – dried garden sage (*Salvia officinalis*), mugwort (*Artemisia vulgaris*) and holy sage (*A. tridentia*), among others, should all roll into fluffy bundles which can hold a spark and smoulder. This scented smoke becomes an offering as it rises and will carry your thoughts from one world into another. In some traditions, the shaman even sends her own spirit out with the smoke from a fire to find the path from this world to that of the spirits.

Grounding

At the end of a session, take a few minutes to:

☆ Stop. Feel the floor beneath you, the room around you, the clothes upon you, your breath within you and your self within you.

☆ Thank the spirits, thank the world.

☆ Snuff out your candle – or let it burn down as a continuing gift – and let any incense fade away.

☆ Stand up and walk around.

Anchor yourself back in the everyday world with a cup of tea and a biscuit or a glass of water. If you keep a journal, sit down and write up the notes of your latest experience.

Always make sure that these sessions have a clear beginning and end. The simplest of actions might suffice, but make sure you separate work 'out there' from life 'back here'.

EXERCISE: TOUCHING STILLNESS

The first skills you need to develop if you are to begin to listen to the world, are the abilities to be still, quiet, aware and to listen. Our lives tend to be full of noise and bustle, and even at rest we are usually watching TV, listening to music or chatting to friends in a pub or club. You need to learn to relax and simply be still, to distract your busy mind from constantly bouncing from one image to another. When you become still, you stand a greater chance of hearing whatever the world may be trying to tell you.

☆ Find somewhere quiet and comfortable to sit, where you will not be disturbed for 20 minutes or so. Settle yourself; some people sit in an upright chair, others cross-legged on a cushion (using another cushion or a wall to support your back can help) or even lying on the floor. Turn off the lights or draw the curtains, maybe light a candle. Close your eyes. The aim is to let your mind relax, to slide away from always thinking about things and let yourself drift in a gentle stillness, an opening for other work to begin.

☆ Breathe – gently, regularly. Do not try to breathe especially deeply or hold your breath for long periods. Find a comfortable length and depth of breath. As you breathe in, feel that breath reaching throughout your body, marking places of tension. As you breathe out, feel the tension release with the air from your body. On the next breath, there should be less tension to release. As you breathe in, 'feel' your thoughts, all those buzzing, endless, incessant images, ideas, worries and 'things I should have said'. As you breathe out, release these as well. Try not to fall asleep.

☆ To finish, open your eyes. Look around. Stand up and walk around for a while. Do something that brings you back down to earth gently: make a cup of tea or a slice of toast perhaps.

This technique takes time and practice, and even after much experience, there will be times when everyday thoughts are as persistent as mosquitoes. The answer is not to try to quell them, because you then concentrate on getting rid of them and that sets everything off again. Relax them away; let them come, see them, feel them, and let them buzz away. Relax.

Sometimes it can help to give yourself a count: perhaps a count of ten breaths, with each breath-cycle relaxing you more. Allow the count to be the only thing you think about; a calm, slow voice in your mind. You may find the count gets slower and slower and stops before you reach ten. If so, great. If not, don't give up!

Variations

☆ You might try counting your in and out breaths: five counts in, hold for five, out for five.

☆ You might add very gentle music, and allow that to provide a background of relaxing sound for your breathing. Sometimes this helps, distracting your mind and tricking it into relaxing. However, it can give you something to fix upon so you find yourself anticipating what will come next and not really relaxing at all.

☆ You might work with an image. Imagine your mind as a pool, with thoughts as bubbles rising from the depths. Watch the bubbles slow and stop and the pool become tranquil. Or imagine your relaxing mind is a field of opening flowers, with stillness spreading as buds unfold across the field; or as a rockpool of clear water with gently waving seaweed lulling you into contemplation.

EXERCISE: VISUALISATION

If you use images to help you relax, you will start to exercise the muscles of your imagination which will be valuable as you move further into shamanism. As a shaman you need to be able to experience things that are not physically present, and a strong imagination is a good starting point. If you can see a forest in your thoughts, for example, feel it around you, hear the wind in it, then you will be better equipped for stepping out of the ordinary world and into the world of the spirits.

☆ Give yourself images to play with. Choose a small scene, or a familiar object (have it in front of you if possible so you can sneak a quick glance now and then) and see it in your thoughts. Your relaxed mind should be a dark stage on to which you can place and spotlight anything you choose: a candle, a houseplant, a cup and saucer. Do not be surprised if living things like plants appear slightly different; colours often change and they may even seem to glow a little. Do not worry. You are simply beginning to see those things with other eyes, picking up on the energies that infuse them but that we do not usually perceive.

EXERCISE: CULTIVATING STILLNESS

You need to cultivate your stillness, and this discipline in itself is often rewarding.

☆ Simply stop for 10 or 15 minutes every day (don't overdo it – once a day or every other day is fine – but do make the commitment to practise). You will find this becomes deliciously therapeutic, with rewards that have little to do with enchantment and a lot to do with true peace and quiet.

☆ Give yourself some variety: vary the time and place if possible. Once you start feeling confident, try working outside, in the garden, the backyard, a city square or on a park bench.

☆ Stop, relax, open your eyes and look around while keeping your mind still. This is a balancing act because you start receiving lots of images to respond to at once. Persevere. Learn to enjoy simply watching or listening or smelling or feeling.

☆ Discover how easy it is to become invisible, both to humans and to animals. The still person gives out very few 'signals' and you may find yourself as background scenery for small birds or be captivated by a spider spinning a web in a nearby bush. Enjoy the world.

2

The Shaman's World

Descriptions of traditional shamanism, with its ice-bound initiations, mountain-top vigils, blood-letting, dangerous drugs and wild trance dances, may leave you wondering why anyone would choose to be a shaman. One response, of course, is that people do not *choose* to become shamans; they are chosen by their community and by the spirits. But you may still be left wondering what the shaman gets out of all of this. You might expect power and influence but that is not always the case, nor does the shaman always receive respect from his clients or a place of privilege among his people. When the shamans speak of their world, however, you can begin to understand what this world of spirits and enchantment brings them. Modern shamans speak of their sense of obligation, of being bound to people, but they reveal other sides to their experiences and speak of a delight in, and a passion for, life that inspires them and fills and fires everything they do. A shaman lives a life where he is always 'falling into wonder'.

This passion for life brings the shaman into a world of connections; a crazy spider's web of bonds that reach out and touch everything around him. They radiate beyond the immediate links of person to tree, bird, wall, plate or dog, to touch and unite everything in the world and beyond it. To a shaman 'all things are connected', and consequently 'whatever befalls the earth befalls the sons of the earth'. Awareness of these connections comes slowly, a growing revelation that develops through personal work and relationships with the world.

In ecology, we talk of 'food webs', drawing patterns that show how each organism in an environment is connected to its prey, the food of that prey, its own predators and the physical environment that all these organisms depend upon. The shaman experiences a similar sense of connectedness, but the web is one of 'spirit', of the energy that inspires life, and its scope is not limited by boundaries of feeding relationships or habitat. The 'Web of life' reaches out to all that we recognise in the world about us as well as to the spirits. That sense of connection is described differently in different cultures: the Web of Wyrd, the Medicine Wheel, the Beauty Way, the Tao, rivers of light. In this book, we shall simply call it the 'Web', a term describing how we are connected rather than a finite thing in itself.

To a shaman, the Web is the force of all the life of this planet, unfolding slowly over the centuries; it is the strength of the planet as a whole, growing, changing and evolving. Strands of the Web may be broken, or their movement halted, but the Web as a whole spins on. It is never still, never stopped. The pathfinder's trails through life are therefore routes across the Web, lines of connections for a community to follow that bring them safely through the maze with as little disturbance and as much harmony as possible. Often the deepest commitment a shaman can express is his commitment to the Web, to protect its movement, or those parts of the whole Web that he can see. Usually those will be 'human' areas, the connections that we make with the world, and those of our immediate environment.

'All That Exists Lives'

In these four words (from J. Halifax's *Shaman: The Wounded Healer*) a Siberian Chukchee shaman summed up the heart of the shamanic world. To a shaman, everything on the Web of life and spirit has an awareness, a consciousness that he can, sometimes, communicate with. You may yourself recognise the presence of a spirit, or a soul, in others, and sometimes in animals. However, for a shaman that perception touches everything and the presence of 'spirit' is recognised everywhere: in stones, wind, rain, houses, people, animals and trees. You may have felt the character of a house as friendly, happy, sad or angry, and put it down to an 'atmosphere'; a shaman would see the house as having a spirit of its own, an awareness grown out of wood, stone and brick, and the accumulated experience of the lives lived within those walls, and would expect to find ways to touch that character, that spirit, directly.

The forms that 'spirit' takes are varied, and when a shaman says that he sees 'spirit' in a stone, he does not necessarily mean that he expects it to speak to him. The stone might do that, or it might not notice him at all, but the shaman will acknowledge its right to be in this world at this time. He recognises its place as part of the Web.

A shaman knows that the spirit people are around us all the time, busy about their own lives, ignoring us, helping us or irritated by us. You could live your life constantly watching and worrying about who you might be treading on, or whose air you might be breathing, but this would make getting on with your own life almost impossible! Just as you do not usually try to interact with everyone you see on a crowded street, so the shaman learns not to be constantly aware of all the spirit activity around him.

It is easier for the shaman if he separates his meetings with the spirits from his everyday life. So shamans speak of the 'spirit world', the Otherworld, a land where shamans, and others, can walk with and talk to the spirits around us. In reality, the Otherworld *is* all around you, beside you all the time. To enter the Otherworld is to open up a set of senses that allow you to look at the familiar world in different ways. It is more than this world with a rosy tint, however; it is a place of dreams and shifting geography, not fixed in any way. You enter it initially through the power of your imagination, but when you become used to its ways you start to experience it as a blend of the dreams and experiences of other beings and of the land itself. Different traditions organise the spirit world in different ways; there may simply be 'this world' and 'the Otherworld', or there may be a 'middle world' (us), and Upper- and Underworlds, Heavens and Hells, even layers and layers of different worlds. In the Nordic tradition, these layers are connected to each other by the World Tree that grows through all the layers making a single whole out of the many parts.

The aspiring shaman must learn the skills that will allow him to walk between the worlds to reach out and meet with the spirits.

The Spiral Path

One image that might describe the course of a shaman's training is that of the Spiral Path. This double spiral represents the two paths that a shaman learns to walk simultaneously: one path winding inward to the heart of the pattern, the other leading out from the centre, to release from the labyrinth and to freedom in the world. The inward path is also the path of the self; the shaman must be able to walk into his own heart, to meet his fears and hopes and ambitions, know his passions, pleasures and pains, and learn to enjoy himself for who he is and for who his spirit is trying to become, not for who other people want him to be. The second path leads the shaman outwards, into the wider

The Spiral Path

world, the world of the spirits and the Web, and into a relationship with a world that is awake and watching him.

Following the Spiral Path is not a straightforward process of walking all the way along one path before stepping on to the other. The shaman learns by walking both paths at the same time, looking deeper and deeper into himself while simultaneously emerging into the world. The two processes are not mutually exclusive; exploring the world can reveal hidden wonders of the self so that the shaman finds himself further along the inward path than expected when next he treads that path.

Walking the Spiral Path challenges and transforms the apprentice shaman. He will encounter aspects of himself he could never have imagined, stand up for himself in front of creatures that seem to have escaped from wicked fairy stories, and immerse himself in the connections of the Web, releasing himself, for a time, to move in the ebb and flow of its wonder. For most modern shamans, the end result of this is that sense of 'falling into wonder', of meeting a world that is so full of enchantment and delight that life suddenly holds an endless source of richness and joy.

Mapping the Otherworld

From his point of entry into the Otherworld, be it smoke hole, World Tree or sacred space, the shaman gradually builds up a picture of the geography of the spirit world. Otherworld landscapes do not obey the rules of geography that we are used to. Distance and terrestrial direction are not as important here as the *way* in which the shaman is travelling. He may travel across the Otherworld as himself, in animal form, give himself to the wind or water, or gather sunlight and radiate golden light. Any one of these would allow him to travel to places in the Otherworld that he is unlikely to reach by other means.

Sometimes the shaman's discoveries are mapped in paint on the skin of a drum, on a shield or embroidered on to a robe or blanket. They become *aides-mémoire* for the shaman and possible guides for apprentices or a watching community. They can also become divination tools, with which the shaman can track the movement of a stray human soul or an errant disease spirit before setting off in pursuit. They might even serve as short cuts for the shaman himself. Meditating upon a track drawn on the skin of his drum, he can sometimes enter the track directly, arriving suddenly at the 'house of the spirits' in question faster than he would otherwise have done.

In building maps for himself, an apprentice shaman can work outwards from his sacred space. If the shaman faces different directions or invites different elements to move with him, he can start to map both form (animal or elemental shape, or energy of movement) and destination (where does that form take him?). He may look at how an element touches his space – the breath of wind on the grass – and may turn to look into that wind and see what it wakes in him, or turn his back to that wind and let it blow through him, transforming him and discovering which qualities its touch wakes in himself.

Old and New Shamans

In our modern technological society, we may not be at the mercy of the elements as our ancestors were. Few of us worry about finding our prey, or whether the salmon will run in the river again. We live in a society that seems to be determined to shut us away from the world as much as it can. But we still need our shamans. Shamans helped their community move harmoniously through the world, disturbing the threads of the Web as little as possible. They helped their people be at ease in their world, and it is these needs that modern societies are recognising once again. A shamanic 'peace' is not a passive condition of complete tranquillity and detachment, but an active, dynamic, passionate relationship with the world. The shaman's world recognises the need for death as much as the value of life. The peace or harmony a shaman may find is a lively one that brings an unfolding awareness of the world and holds respect for the other spirits who live on this earth and respect for that earth itself.

In the past, a shaman and his people would have shared the same worldviews. The language they used to describe the world around them would have been the same, whether that spoke of spirits, devils, demons or angels. A modern shaman is likely to work with people who see the world in a wide variety of ways, who might think of the shaman's world as strange, to say the least, but who have come to him because he offers the skills they need. A shaman does not dictate or control what you believe or how you are, but helps you to listen to your own spirits and to the world around you. An effective shaman will try to find a path to peace with the self and with the planet that people can use within their own faith.

Sometimes a shaman's clients may have no awareness of the spiritual nature of the shaman's work, but come to him because he sings, dances, makes things, heals, or helps people to change. The shaman may be inspired by the spirits, while the client is not interested, or would be horrified by such thoughts, but trusts the shaman to find a way towards some measure of joy or harmony. It is also worth remembering that a shaman's work is never done. Shamans are unlikely to find final answers to anything. If a shaman finds a path for a person to follow, they may only be able to guide them along a few steps of that path; the track will unfold as the person walks along it. Look upon life as a journey along a road or a woodland trail: the track runs on for as long as you are alive, and perhaps afterwards as well. The shaman's task may have been simply to point out the first landmark, to open the gate, or he might turn up every so often like a useful signpost at moments of confusion. A shaman may be a pathfinder and a guide, but the path a person walks is his own, changing with the choices he makes, and never ends within his life.

To live in a shamanic world, you do not need to be a shaman. While in some traditional shamanic societies, only the shaman can have contact with the spirit world, in others, most members of the community are aware of their own relationship with the spirits. Individuals and families have their own spirit guides and totems, ceremonies that they will perform, and obligations to the spirits that they will honour. They only turn to the shaman when they need extra guidance. It is rather like a modern community's relationship with its doctors or counsellors. We can all look after ourselves on a day-to-day basis, dealing with personal issues, ailments or celebrations as they arise, but when things feel too serious or are getting out of hand, or when we want that extra guidance and experience that the 'expert' brings, we look for professional advice. So people in our society might still explore their relationships with, obligations to and celebrations of a living world without taking on the extra responsibility or trying to find the skills that make them shamans, and a book such as this remains useful in developing such relationships. The qualities that go to make up a shaman may prove useful in all of us.

The Modern Community

Shamans work in many different ways, fulfilling a number of roles within communities. Even when shamans were bound to smaller communities, while any shaman might be expected to be a 'jack of all trades', there were some who were better healers, or water-finders, or hunting guides than others. Modern shamans are still 'jacks', but there are also specialists in areas appropriate to the time. In general, modern shamans fall into three main groups:

(1) **Healers** help people listen to themselves and their own spirit, and to move with harmony in their own lives.
(2) **Speakers** help individuals and groups, listen to themselves, and help to heal the bonds within communities.
(3) **Patterners** help communities explore their relationships with nature and smooth the way between people and environment again.

The **tricksters** are still around too, as healer, speaker or patterner, and troublemaker. Whatever the role, a shaman helps people within communities to listen: to each other, to themselves as individuals, and to the world.

Becoming a Shaman

To become a shaman, you need to learn to walk the Spiral Path, to follow both inward and outward journeys, and explore yourself and your relationships with the world. Even in well-established traditions, a shamanic training was often as much about attitudes and principles as practical 'things to learn and do'. While different cultures would have their own recognised ways in which a shaman might work, a shamanic language of ceremony and behaviour as it were, how the shaman spoke that language was often very much up to him.

In our world, the language of shamanism is fragmented. We are finding new words and borrowing phrases from other languages as we go along. There is a danger of creating a pile of gibberish that no-one understands, particularly if we focus too much on the words (the ceremonies, tools, exotic practices), and forget the meaning behind them (the reasons for speaking). So, while this book will introduce you to some of the language used by modern shamans, it will look more closely at the meanings those words are trying to convey, so that in the end you will be able to choose your own words, rather than relying upon mine or anyone else's.

There are five key qualities that you should find in most shamans, whether they describe themselves as speakers, healers, patterners or some other term. These are:

(1) **Honesty:** in himself as a person, accepting the diversity of emotions, skills and ideas that makes him as unique as every other individual.
(2) **Integrity:** the personal strength that forges relationships with spirits of all kinds.
(3) **Vision:** a readiness to stop and listen to the Infinite, to touch the patterns of the Web.
(4) **Humility:** with all his strength and vision, he will still be called to awe by the wonder of the world and the gods and goddesses of the Infinite.
(5) **Passion:** all the above are reached through passion, for shamanism is a world of ecstasy; that awe in the world may be humbling but it is also engulfing and ferocious.

A shamanic training does not, however, make you a shaman. Other people do that. You become a shaman by finding that you are doing the job, being a pathfinder, acting as the bridge between the worlds, used by people to find a path towards a harmony with the world and used by the spirits to smooth the passage of humanity through the rest of the world.

EXERCISE: SACRED SPACE

One of the first tasks on the Spiral Path is finding your own gateway into that Otherworld of the spirits. You need to create for yourself a place that will become your crossing-over point from this world to the Otherworld. This 'sacred space' will be a working site when you are in that world, a sanctuary, and a quick route home if ever you need it. It will be the place where the two worlds meet and from which you can venture out to explore the Otherworld.

The idea of using a sacred space as the meeting point between the physical and Otherworld is just one way for a shaman to move between the worlds. Native traditions have developed many other ways of entering the spirit realms: climbing Yggdrasil, the World Tree of Norse mythology and stepping out from its broad branches into any of the Nine Worlds; following the smoke of wood and fat burned in a fire with your spirit flying with the smoke out of the smokehole in the roof and off into the night; standing on top of a carved pole, another World Tree, looking out beyond the walls of the physical world; the steady pulse of drum and rattle lulls you into the floating darkness of a ceremony where, as dancing lights, the spirits come. For now we shall stick with the idea of 'sacred space'. You can go on to explore other ways of travelling as you become more experienced.

☆ Think of some outdoor place where you felt safe and peaceful. It might be a secret place from your childhood or a woodland glade you still visit today. You do not need a detailed, conscious knowledge of this place, more the general shape of it and the feelings it woke in you. It does not need to be somewhere wild and remote, a quiet corner in a local park is just as good. You are going to give the memory of that place substance, first in your imagination and then in the Otherworld itself.

☆ Prepare yourself as we described in the Touching Stillness exercise (see page 17). Set up some music and incense, or light a candle or two. Make yourself comfortable and relax. This time, as you settle into that relaxed state, you are going to reach out to find a new world around you.

☆ Use the relaxing sequence from the Touching Stillness exercise to start you drifting and then call your special place into being around you. Feel the textures: the ground beneath you, a breeze that touches you; smell the flowers or the stream; sense the dappling of light through leaves on your skin.

☆ Breathe. On the in breath, hold the picture firm, on the out breath allow it to grow. Watch the mist flow back. Do not hurry or push it. Let the mist go with your breath and watch the boundaries of your space form around you.

☆ When you feel that you have done as much as you can, rest in that space. Hold the image. Treasure it. Then let yourself dissolve into mist and come back to the everyday world.

It will probably take a number of sessions before you have revealed all of your space. Do not worry if you 'feel' rather than 'see' things; perceiving the Other-world can take many forms. As before, do not rush it, enjoy relaxing and looking at the little changes of each session. Do not be surprised if the space is not quite as you remember it. Enjoy it for what it is. You are a trainee shaman now, working with the world, not upon it, and anything once shaped needs to be respected for what it might choose to become.

Developing Your Sacred Space

With practice, the process of waking the shape of your place around you will become smoother. The step from here to there will become easier and your sacred space will become a familiar, comfortable place to step into. Take time to explore it. In your thoughts, see yourself get up and walk around. Touch things. Feel things. Renew the thrill of contact when you stroke the bark of a tree or the flank of a stone. Be comfortable here.

Think of your sacred space as a doorway between the everyday world and the Otherworld. This is your threshold. It is also your sanctuary because it is a place that you have shaped yourself. Somewhere out there will be the 'original' that your version is based upon, but this space has come from your thoughts, memories and imagination. It is yours. For now, no-one else may enter without your permission, and wherever you go in the Otherworld, you will hold the image, the coordi-nates, of your sacred space in your heart and will be able to call up that image with a thought and be back there with the pulse of your blood.

With time, explore your sacred space from different directions. Try being blown in by a north wind or a southern breeze. See if different animals or plants respond or which colours come to mind when different breezes blow.

Over time, all these factors will change a little as your sacred space settles into the Otherworld landscape. You may find the plants flowering or the trees in leaf unexpectedly as it starts to live its own life. This can seem alarming, as if you are losing control, but it is also a measure of the sacred space's strength; it is taking root, becoming part of that world, and you will need less and less effort to find it for yourself. It is always there, still private, still yours, but growing into the magic of the Otherworld.

3

Tools of the Trade

From South American jungle to Siberian steppe, Australian desert to South African scrub, wherever shamanism occurs, shamans have developed a bewildering array of tools and techniques to allow them to travel between the worlds. All have found their own distinctive ways of opening the door between the worlds and allowing themselves to meet the spirits.

Where a teacher is leading workshops or some other training system based upon the techniques of another culture, this may offer a ready-made set of practices for the trainee; the apprentice shaman may find ways of accessing her own relationship with land and spirits through techniques that evolved in other lands. Sometimes, however, such shamanic techniques are taught in defiance of the elders or shamans of the original culture. Claims of 'global relevance' and 'world harmony' are used to justify the pillaging of other people's cultural identities, picking odd combinations of attractive techniques and appealing ideas from a range of cultures to create a nondescript whole that might offer a certain solace and feeling of achievement through the excitement of drums or the drama of ritual, but which has no wider relevance or context to draw people, place and spirit into closer communication. There is much middle ground between such positions, but the aspiring shaman needs to look carefully at what is being offered in workshops, who and where it comes from ('I was taught by this Lakota/Inca/Siberian shaman, the best of his/her kind') and what connection it offers with the land she is walking on now.

If you look at original practices, read accounts of their use, and listen to first-hand descriptions from across the world, you will find that there are some basic similarities in the way different shamans work. Underneath the kaleidoscope of tools and ceremonies are working techniques that can be found over and over again. Lifting these out of the detail of different ceremonies can offer you the backbone of a technical skeleton around which to build a modern shamanic animal.

Techniques used by shamans fall into a number of general groups: song and other voice work; dance or other movement; music from instruments; the use of drugs and 'teacher plants'; application of pain; stillness. If a range of ceremonies is examined, these components can be found in a variety of combinations. Song, dance and music may each stand alone or work in combination. Ceremonies may be private, performed by the shaman alone or with only one or two people present, or may take place in front of a small group or a whole community. The observers may be passive witnesses of the event or be actively involved in the whole process. The permutations are endless and it is up to the individual shaman to find the components that she works most comfortably with.

Tools

It is worth taking care to separate the *tools* of the shaman from her *techniques*. A rattle is a tool used in a musical way, but you might explore the same technique with other tools. There is little that is so precious it cannot be changed. Shamans are wonderful improvisers and I have come across rituals conducted by respected traditional shamans using fire-lighters and half a fizzy drinks can. Shamans do not sacrifice the technique in the desire for the right tools – the right tool is often whatever the shaman can lay her hands on at the time.

Bundles and Power Objects

As a shaman works, she gradually accumulates a selection of tools. Some may be the familiar rattles and drums, while others may be small plastic animals, shards of sea-polished glass or collections of odd bits and pieces, stalked, found and bound together with string because of a set of connections the shaman and her spirits can detect within them. These are fetishes, 'power objects', things touched by the spirit world. When a shaman makes and uses a fetish, she draws together items that bring the spirits to her. A fetish becomes a minia-ture gateway through which the shaman and the spirits can work towards particular ends. With use, a fetish accumulates its own residual energy; it becomes a battery, if you like, and on picking it up the shaman can draw upon that power supply without always reaching out to the spirits beyond. A 'bear fetish', for example, will invite Bear spirits to work with that shaman and she might then dance Bear with extra insight or be possessed more readily by Bear in a profound healing trance. In her hands, however, that bear fetish alone might be especially effective as a healing tool.

A number of fetishes held together become a 'bundle', a collection of power objects, wrapped up in cloth or leather or held safe in a box. Some bundles are personal to the shaman, while others represent bodies of teaching and grow over the years, or even centuries, that they are in use. Bundles are sacred things, guarded and kept safe until they are called upon to open and reveal their power.

Techniques

Tools are details, but a technique is one of the six basic approaches to entering a trance that will carry the shaman into the Otherworld. No matter how varied the techniques employed by different shamans, they all serve essentially the same purpose. A shaman uses the appropriate technique at any one time to allow her to open the gates to the Otherworld and bring her to a place and to spirits who are appropriate for the task in hand. A shaman's techniques are her 'paths to ecstasy'. They are designed to provide sound, movement, or other stimuli that allow the shaman to step out of her everyday world, releasing her own spirit from those concerns to travel in the spirit realms. Shamanic techniques create a sense of heightened awareness in their user, opening their eyes to the worlds beyond the everyday. Sometimes an entranced shaman is a quiet, almost passive person, while at other times the shaman's voice sings the wonders she is seeing or her body dances the emotions of her travels. Watching a shaman work is often one of the best ways of understanding the passion: with the drums behind her or the teacher plants within her, a shaman gives herself completely to the experiences of her Otherworld journey.

Even in the middle of the whirling frenzy, these techniques are also about stillness. When she is entranced, a shaman may be whirling round the room but deep inside herself, her spirit steps out of the movement and, standing in grace and stillness, listens to the world speaking. In typical shamanic fashion, the shaman needs both: the headlong ecstasy of song, music and dance, and the ability to be utterly still within that.

In this chapter we will focus on the six essential shamanic techniques. Some of the tools that might be used to pursue these techniques will be encountered later, as will some of the ceremonies that a modern shaman might design to develop their shamanic work.

Song

Song and dance are two of the shaman's most fundamental techniques. Nothing is required but the body of the shaman, and while they may be complemented by costume, head-dress and the power of medicine bundles, their essence is simple and straightforward.

A shaman sings a *powersong*, often a personal song found through Vision, that will carry her from this world into the Otherworld. The words and rhythm of a song become shapes, a ladder for the shaman's spirit to climb, a gate for the shaman to open, and a cry to the spirits that a shaman is coming. The power of traditional songs often does not lie in their melody, or even their words, but in their repetition. Indeed many do not have words as such but 'vocables', sounds without explicit meanings that are used like words and chosen for the effect their sound and their vibration has on body and spirit. Traditional powersongs are usually short and simple and repeated over and over again. Whether sung, chanted, or spoken with rhythm, a shaman and her spirit family all recognise the words and shape of a powersong as a prelude to work. The spirits will gather as they hear the singing, while the shaman can use the chanted repetition as a way of relaxing her mind and slipping into stillness, feeling the words of the chant as a river that lifts the boat of her spirit, carrying her away and sweeping her home again when the work is done.

Sometimes powersongs are very private, sung only and known only by their shaman owner, while at other times participants at a ceremony may be expected to join the shaman in her song. A shaman can then stop singing and slip away and the song will continue, her people supporting her, strengthening her and at length giving her a direct route home again with the sound of their voices.

Dance

When a shaman dances, she dances in all the worlds at once. Her turning body spins in this world and the Otherworld, her stamping feet follow paths seen among the spirits or trace patterns of power moving through the earth. The dancing shaman may be festooned with things of power – a robe decorated with tokens from her spirit family, memories of other adventures, or a cap or head-dress of feathers that brings the flight of geese or the night-eyes of owls into her travelling. A dancing shaman in full outfit is a spectacular sight and might be seen, cynically, as a colourful confirmation for a community that their shaman is 'out there, doing her stuff and looking strange and mysterious'. It is only in the Otherworld that the full impact of a dance costume is seen; feathers and bones, metal, stone and fur, the spectacle and decoration swirl with the dancer, following her movement, drawing patterns in the air – flaring patterns of power, like the after-images of bright lights and fireworks, an explosion of sparks and flowing rainbows.

Shamanic dances may use long-established steps or ways of movement. Like a song or a drumbeat, a simple set of steps may be repeated, their effect lying in the repetition, setting up a rhythm in the body that allows the shaman to stop thinking about the dance and allows every step to take her farther from home. Some of these dances are passed down over generations and taught to new shamans or to whole communities. In the West these are known as 'folk dances' and we often laugh at them a little, but when danced with excitement and passion they can capture something of the delight and potency of a whole community dancing together. Not all folk dances are 'shamanic' dances by any means. They serve many purposes, from solemn ritual to straightforward community celebration, but now and then we come across dances whose repeated steps carry us away so that we dance without thinking and our dancing bodies still and relax our spirits. Yet other dances are more 'free-form'. From simple beginnings they may grow into passionate adventures, with the story of the shaman's encounters being played out through her body. Watchers will not see the detail of these incidents, but may read the emotions of those moments in her dance.

Like the other techniques, a shaman's dance actually brings stillness. The passion of these movements and the ecstasy of the dance is very real, but the dancing also sets the spirit free to stand still and wondering in the eye of the dancer's storm. And later, when she is off doing other everyday things, a dancing shaman finds that the dance goes on inside her; in the still space at the heart of her life, the dancer goes on dancing.

Music

Pick up a drum and hit it, take up a rattle and shake it, and become a shaman! Instruments are often seen as the *sine qua non* of the shaman's craft, but they are really only one option in the shaman's repertoire. A shaman needs to be able to work with a range of techniques and tools, choosing those which seem appropriate for a particular situation, for example, drum, voice or teacher plant, but she also needs to be able to operate without any of her familiar tools at times, or even to improvise wildly. We are not bound by any convention that tells us all shamans use rattles, or a fashion that expects everyone to play a *djembe* this year while we were all playing *bodhrans* last year.

Like the voice, instruments give us rhythm, creating a river of sound to carry the shaman into the Otherworld, and as with song, this might be a private occasion, or a powerful way in which a community can support their shaman in her work. In some places, trance dancers, for example, can only dance when the village sings the songs and plays the tunes that let the spirits dance.

Traditional shamans are not restricted to familiar drums and rattles. Percussion of one sort or another does tend to dominate the shamanic orchestra, but while it might be hand-held rattles, it could also be shells, hooves or moth cocoons strapped on to the body, strings of bells on a dance costume, or pierced coins on the edge of a head-dress. Carved sticks and painted stones call the clattering rhythms of water, rain and running insects, while other shamans use horns to call the spirits in, or didgeridoos to wake the earth.

A shaman's music, like a chant, can be very simple, inducing trance by repetition, a throbbing background with which to pace travel in the Otherworld and to guide a shaman home again. The complicated layers of African drum rhythms may suit some people better, while others may use the plaintive sound of a fiddle to evoke an emotional atmosphere as they work.

A traditional shaman probably works with the instruments and rhythms that belong to her society, however, a modern shaman must find the rhythms that she, her people and her spirits respond to. Both traditional and modern workers now draw upon modern technology and use recorded music in their work, and anything from classical symphonies to New Age compositions and Gothic rock is being used to pace travel and support dance trances.

Drugs and Teacher Plants

The use of mind-altering, usually plant-derived, drugs has been one of the most widely promoted traditional shamanic practices and, alongside drums and rattles, seems to be an expected part of every shaman's repertoire. Perhaps because our technological society tends to frown upon the use of recreational and religious drugs as opposed to 'medicinal' ones, traditional shamanic drugs are often pounced upon as much because they are forbidden, and thus attractive, as because the user has been called to them by the plant spirits that stand behind them.

'Teacher plant' is a title given in some traditional cultures to certain plants which are recognised as being especially effective agents for inducing trance and for taking a shaman on powerful journeys. While many plants are known to have curative or other useful properties only a few ever become identified as 'teachers' and their use is carefully controlled.

The teacher plants are very powerful, and the drugs that are derived from their extracts open routes into Otherworlds that may be wildly different from those entered by other means. These worlds are full of colour and changing perspectives, deeply surreal experiences and, at times, numbing horrors. The effects of *peyote* (from a cactus) or *yahe* (from a vine) or fly agaric toadstools might be dismissed as simple psychotropic adventures, but in the hands of an experienced shaman, the teacher plants themselves will meet the traveller and through their influence she will encounter spirits rarely met elsewhere and experience a world of awareness and consciousness far in excess of the basic chemical influences.

Teacher plants are very powerful but they are also very dangerous. They defend their mysteries carefully and the consequences of crossing them by inappropriate use of their derivatives can be formidable. Their traditional use is almost always under the guidance of an experienced shaman and is never lightly undertaken, no matter how informal the description of a session may sound. Their use needs to be approached with great care and respect and is not recommended for beginners, certainly not without the guidance of a shaman experienced in their use.

Pain

In a culture that tends to do its best to avoid pain, it can seem peculiar, or even illegal, to expose oneself willingly to pain as a spiritual practice. But some shamanic societies do just that: rituals are conducted in which pain allows the shaman to separate body from spirit and send the spirit travelling into the Otherworld. Where song or music might create the river current that takes the shaman away, here pain achieves the same end.

At other times, pain is seen as the price a shaman must pay for her activities: a measure of her commitment to her cause.

That at least has similarities in our everyday world, particularly in sport where 'no pain, no gain' is a familiar cry. But the piercing sun-dances of some American First Nations, the thorn and tongue divinations of the old Maya, the ice-bound visions of Siberian shamans all recognise pain itself as a valid path to trance and enlightenment.

Allowing yourself to experience pain in the course of a ceremony is a form of sacrifice, echoing the thought that in the end all you have is yourself and all you can offer is yourself. After dance, song, music, art and feasts have been used, your body remains as the gift that you can offer your world. Dance and song especially are offerings of flesh and spirit combined, and your pain may be part of that gift. Blood too is the pulse of life, and some modern shaman craftsmen may offer blood from a slashed hand in return for wood taken from a tree; a pierced thumb may bleed on to a leather robe or rawhide rattle; or a dancer's heel may be cut open by her ankle bells in the passion of the dance.

The conscious pursuit of pain is a delicate quest and not one recommended to the apprentice shaman. Incidental pain is accepted, however, and even explored: an aching body may signify a vigorous dance, a cut catches you as you carve a piece of wood. These things happen when they need to happen, when you need to recognise what you do. In everyday living, you take from the world and in return you offer yourself to the world, and your pain may be your recognition of the gift you have received, your blood sealing the exchange that is made. But all these things are done because they are the right thing to do, not because everyone is watching and you want to impress them. Most 'voluntary' pain in modern shamanism happens in private and is not part of public performance or discussion: wood gathering, or a hunting dance that has hammered the shaman into the floor are usually things that the shaman does alone and no-one may ever know the offering she made during her work.

When you read fierce and bloody accounts of traditional ceremonies look at these with a shaman's eyes and ask yourself if the pain is being used as a tool to induce trance, or is it being used as a way of simply impressing or intimidating people. Sometimes, however, letting their blood flow in a ceremony is the only offering a person feels they can give: when you have nothing to offer the world but yourself you may give back to the earth something of the life, the blood in your veins, that the earth has already given you. Keep this in mind before you start hiding from some of the grimmer traditional ceremonies. Shamanism does not happen in a room labelled 'comfortable': look at the reasons for actions and recognise that as you discover your own language for talking with the earth, similar things may be expected of you.

Stillness

At the beginning of this chapter, I said that techniques found in traditional shamanism are also about stillness. The vigour and excitement of the practices help the shaman move into a deep inner stillness, a time of awareness that may coincide with or may follow livelier activities. People tend to expect shamanism to be 'active': the songs, music, drugs and dances are the recognised face of this world, but stillness plays a powerful part in its own right. Times of quiet contemplation and deep trance are all used in traditional shamanism, and this ability to be still is so fundamental that it is often not even mentioned. Shamans have to know how to be silent on the inside, to shut up voice, body and conscious mind. From Visionquest and Vigil to quiet consideration of a client's health problems, a shaman must be able to stop, listen and let her spirit within and the spirits beyond speak without the interference of ego and conscious thoughts. You will need to cultivate stillness. It is a rare quality in Western society and will become the core of your regular communion with the Otherworld as a shaman.

There is a range of techniques for the modern shaman to explore. Some will be more effective for one person than for another and different tools will feel right for different people. When working, a shaman must be aware of what she is doing and why she is doing it, separating intention, technique and tool:

☆ **Intention:** the reason for the activity and its anticipated outcome.

☆ **Technique:** the process by which the shaman will explore that intention.

☆ **Tool:** the individual skill or piece of equipment that is used to conduct that exploration.

With time, the shaman learns to make these decisions almost instinctively. A particular problem will 'feel' like a music ceremony worked with that healing rattle, or that favourite horse rattle or the drum. The shaman has to grow to trust the instinct that identifies techniques and tools as a sense that picks the path across the Web, recognising the ceremony that will help the path to become clear and allow the traveller to move safely again. To begin with, however, the shaman needs to stop, think, and not rush headlong into every situation waving her drum and tripping up on her dance robe. Evolving ways of working and discovering the tools and techniques that you work most comfortably with are good ways of developing your relationship with your spirit family. Sit down together and talk. Listen. Again and again, learn to listen: to the world, to the spirits, to your own heart speaking.

EXERCISE: MUSIC AND SONG

These techniques, or 'paths to ecstasy', are a means through which to provide your mind with a background beat, a rhythm that will help you relax and set yourself free from your everyday thoughts. With experience these techniques can become very complicated: layers of sound, movement, song, pain, drugs and stillness accumulate to create overwhelming ceremonies. At any stage of a shaman's training, however, encountering these practices in their simplest forms can still be effective.

☆ Equip yourself with something which will make a noise: two dry sticks or stones would be ideal, or a bottle half-filled with dry peas, or a child's drum. Traditionally, tools were passed on by a mentor or made by hand. Now, we might buy a rattle or a drum, although many modern shamans still make their own. As this is a first encounter, it is probably more useful to explore the technique before committing yourself to an instrument.

☆ Make sure you will not be interrupted, sit down and start tapping. Give yourself a simple rhythm, something you can repeat time and time again without getting confused. Try to maintain a regular speed to begin with and use that rhythm in your relaxation exercise to pace your breathing. Feel it as a rhythm in your bones. You might find that you start swaying a little (the beginnings of a dance!).

☆ Enter your sacred space with the sound of the rhythm. Find yourself there, still tapping. Hold on to the beat, although now the rhythm might start to change. As you feel the Otherworld around you, the beat may grow faster, rippling, slowing down, or even stopping altogether. If you find that you simply stop, so be it. If your music has brought you to the Otherworld, perhaps it has done its job for now.

☆ As you tap, however, you might feel inspired to add sounds: little calls, grunts, or wailing that adds a sense of fluidity to a staccato beat (hence the importance of being undisturbed). Try not to be embarrassed – have a good laugh by all means but don't shrivel up and cringe!

☆ Add words as they come to you. A good start might be the place you are going to and the people you might meet there. Do not worry about rhyming or sentences, but try to hang on to rhythm. Name the features you will meet as single words repeated, or as phrases: 'Grass, woods, stone, trees/a flower, a leaf, a moss, a dream' or 'Sunlight on leaf/Shadow under stone/Snow in the morning/The wings of birds.'

☆ When it is time to finish, you might use your tapping to bring you back to the everyday world, following the sound as you go through the familiar grounding procedure, or you might use the end of the sound as a cue to stop and return. You could back up your own efforts with recorded music; do not use anything too dramatic, just something you could accompany with your stones that would still give you a rhythm to follow if your own efforts peter out. Taped music can also be used to set the length of a session (15–20 minutes is fine until you feel comfortable with a longer session). Tapes of 'drumming for the shamanic journey' are available as well as exciting recordings of overtone or throat singing, and everything from snail-shell nose-flutes to Lakota pow-wow songs. It is up to you to find what works for you. You will soon know if you find yourself sitting there thinking, 'This stuff sounds awful!'

☆ Clap, slap, tap or beat. Mutter, grumble, speak or sing. Sway. Stand up and shuffle. Stamp a foot rhythm and the dance begins. Experiment. Write it down afterwards. Start to build your own set of tools.

4

Honesty on the Inside

To walk the double spiral of a shaman's path is often to trip and stumble over apparent contradictions. We need to move inward even as we move outward, exploring ourselves as we explore the spirit world opening up around us. That outward journey may seem more adventurous and full of wonders, alarms and strange delights, but the inward journey is just as important to a shaman's skill. Indeed, it is often more challenging. In walking through the Otherworld, you may give yourself to wolves to be eaten, but on the inward path you may have to give yourself to yourself to be eaten. The inward path is also full of marvels, warnings and unexpected pleasures, and it is vital that you can walk it confidently, into the very heart of who you are, for there, at the still centre of yourself, lies the doorway to Vision, where the Universe speaks to your heart and spirit.

The process of exploring yourself is not one that is spoken about very often in the accounts of traditional shamanism. It may be that those shamans did go through a process of self-discovery, or perhaps that process was expected to be contained within their 'outward spiral' work. It is certainly implicit in many accounts of Vision, and the rituals by which a shaman received his Vision. Vision leaves you open, naked before the Infinite, and you need to be strong to face this and to spend time looking at who you have been, while waiting for the revelation that will show who you might become. It is, however, also possible that who you were as an individual was not seen to be of much relevance to your work as a shaman, or that the inward spiral is one of honesty with your-self, and there was not such a great need among those cultures for this to require special consideration.

'Me Myself'

'Me Myself' comes from *The Tale of Fincastle Mill*, a tradi-tional Scottish story, which goes something like this:

> . . . As the girl worked, an ugly little man crept into the kitchen and stood glowering at her. Brownie Clod asked the girl what her name was. 'Oh, I am Me Myself,' she replied . . . . Later, Brownie Clod tried to steal the eggs she had brought for her baking, but the girl rapped him on the hand with a hot spoon. Furious, he leapt on to the table to seize the eggs and she threw a pot of boiling water in his face. Nursed by his mother, the boggart Meg Moulach, Brownie Clod nevertheless died of his injuries. Through all his woes he could only ever tell his mother that 'It was Me Myself that hurted me.'

The answer 'I am Me Myself', often appears in tales as a way of outwitting some boggart or other faerie visitor, but for a shaman it is also a claim that has stronger implications.

The Otherworld is not always a safe place in which to go

adventuring. You may have long periods of calm, peaceful discovery, but at other times you will meet people who seem out to trick you, deceive you, pull off your arms and legs and eat you for breakfast. Some of these may well be Otherworld inhabitants finding their own way of testing your strength and your commitment, but often the things that shake us up most are our own fears and insecurities given shape in the spirit world and reflected back at us as we work in it. Thus the landscape of the inward and outward spirals tends to be much the same: it all happens 'out there' and 'in here' at the same time.

This does not mean that our anxieties become independent of ourselves and lead interesting lives of their own. Rather, think of the Otherworld as a three-dimensional mirror of the heart, reflecting back at us what we bring to it. This is not a direct matching of fear for fear, happiness for happiness, but a reflection that may be best thought of as 'what you hide is what you get' rather than 'what you see is what you get'. You may enter the Otherworld with arrogance or pride and be crippled by fear, you may enter with apparent joy and have your festering anger sprout around you. The Otherworld responds to the heart, spirit and emotion much more than to reasoned discussion. The careful 'front' we present to the world and all the nice 'proper' statements we make, of friendship with the world, accepting spirits as equals, loving and caring for our community, are seen through as the Otherworld responds to what lies in the heart rather than what lies on the tongue. Whatever we hide down deep inside of us will, sooner or later, come walking through the woods towards us.

It is not safe to go walking in the Otherworld, any more than it is safe to cross a busy road or dance down a motorway at rush hour. In everyday life we either take precautions that allow us to do what we must, or sensibly avoid things that are too life-threatening. So it is in our shamanism: like children, we cannot learn to walk unless we go stumbling along and fall over a few times. Some older and more experienced shaman may, like a helpful big sister, be around to hold a hand or dust down a bruised knee, but they cannot learn to walk for us. If you choose to go walking in the Otherworld, you will have to learn to do it for yourself.

When you do step out into the Otherworld, remember that it will be watching, listening, hearing the words you say and the words in your heart and comparing the distance between the two. Lie in the Otherworld and sooner or later something will catch up with you and make you eat your words. As a shaman, you are not a medieval sorcerer, conjuring demons to appear, bound within a ceremonial circle. You are more likely to be out there in the middle of them, where your strongest defence is the line 'I am Me Myself'. 'Me Myself' is a statement of identity, a claim of being who you choose to be, and a defiance of anyone who thinks you should be 'Who I want you to be'. But you must be able to say it from the heart and not just from the head, for the monstrous affliction facing you may well be picking out your fears and throwing them back at you. If you have looked – and are looking – at yourself, if you are walking the inward spiral, your personal horrors become much less alarming and you can confidently answer, 'Yes, I know about this part of me, and no, I have not met my Need For Respectability before, but I can see myself there. And that is all right. I am still Myself.' Knowing who you are is your greatest safety.

The Past

'I am Me Myself' is not a finite statement. You are not claiming that you know yourself inside out and have dismissed, integrated or otherwise dealt with every anxiety and trauma that lurks inside your head. You are claiming that you are exploring who you are, getting to know the insides of yourself, opening boxes, dusting the skeletons in their closets, and generally having an interesting spring clean. The aim is to recognise who you are *now*, reflecting on the individual incidents and connected patterns of the life that have brought you to this place. This is not a time of judgement on how good, bad or indifferent you may have been in the past, but of observing: 'This is what I did' and perhaps 'This is why I did it' and maybe 'If I was there now, I would do something else.' All the things that you have been, that have been done to you, that you have seen, heard or shared in are part of the rich earth of your past. None of them are necessarily better than others, or worse, nicer or nastier. They simply are. Use them to nourish the earth and feed the growing plant of who you are now.

The inward path is not necessarily a path of healing. It may be, and you may discover something that will ease an old wound or issues that still need resolving. Perhaps you can do this for yourself or you may turn to a counsellor, friend or another shaman for advice. There may, however, be other things in those dusty boxes stored in your head; shake them down, have a look and put them away again. You should not expect to answer all your questions or resolve all your issues, but it is valuable to know that they are there.

This process will not free you from emotion. Some people hope that they will become all sweetness, light and joy as shamans. Why? The world is a fierce and vibrant place and a shaman works with passion. That passion may well be full of gentle delight, but the delight might also be danced with howling joy, or rich, rolling, gutsy sensuality, or sharp, fierce anger. Emotions give us variety as people, as communities, making us unpredictable and delightful. As shamans, we need to listen to the emotions that move through us, feel the emotions that wake and try to understand what wakes them, while at the same time trusting them, respecting them, and maybe letting them go rather than acting upon them, or letting ourselves go and being prepared to weep, laugh, dance and sing if that is what allows us to do our jobs better as shamans. The inward spiral takes us into ourselves, into the confusing heart of being human. In becoming shamans, we learn to work with all sorts of other beings. This should help us to operate more effectively as human beings, as creatures of thought, decision and passion. Do not imagine that you will walk this path once and walk away with everything sorted out. We never get to the end of it. There will always be more because new experiences settle on to the leafy compost of our minds, feeding and changing the growing flower of our current self.

Now when you meet some Otherworld inhabitant, you will be better prepared to stop and talk with them. If you can honestly say that you are 'Me Myself' then they are much more likely to treat you as an equal rather than a potential plaything, and you can meet them with confidence and in your honesty see the truth of who they are and hear better the meanings behind their words.

Honour

As a shaman you may have to walk in strange places or do unpleasant things and you will only succeed if you follow your path with all your heart. If you turn up to reclaim someone's lost soul from the beast who ran off with it, you have to be there because you have chosen to come, not because it is someone else's fault. You are not a frightened child saying 'Please, sir, she made me do it!' In the Otherworld, you act because you have chosen to act. This will start to spill over into your everyday life; to be one thing in the Otherworld and another in the physical world defeats all that carefully nurtured honesty.

Your honesty steps into the space between 'I'm angry because she did that' and 'I'm angry because I do not like what she did.' The difference between these statements might seem pedantic but it is an important one. The shaman recognises her own emotions and accepts responsibility for them. She knows that she is affected by what other people do but she does not blame them for how she feels: her anger, joy, sorrow and delight are her own. When you are 'Me Myself' you lay claim to your emotions.

Honesty seems to spread; as you get used to looking shrewdly at what you are doing, you start looking at other people the same way. But you have to learn to be careful and not blurt out the truths you see as obvious in other people's lives. Remember that you may be wrong, that you may be seeing what you would like to see in yourself in other people, or finding what you would like those other people to see in you. You have to learn to step back, to watch, to feel, to measure your evaluation of a situation against what you would like it to be and what the situation itself is trying to be.

The inward spiral is a path of self-awareness, of looking afresh at who you have been and who you are. It is an important part of your preparation, and while it is a process that you will never finish, you will gradually establish ways of 'keeping an eye' on yourself, and discover that outward spiral work, your relationships with the world, also feeds your understanding of yourself. Your honesty supports your integrity; both this world and the Otherworld will come to recognise the clarity with which you act and the essential honesty that underlies your words and actions. Even tricksters, those most elusive and troublesome of shamans, work from a degree of personal honesty, although the world they view and work in can be so different from other people's that their honesty seems a complete inversion of what others expect.

Honesty becomes binding. Shamans do not lightly promise to undertake anything – to break a promise is a blow to your integrity, to the belief you are nurturing within yourself that what you say, you do, and if you can't do it, you don't speak. Honesty gives you personal strength and confidence. It prepares you, as much as anything can, to face the trials of Vision and gives you as much courage as anything can to pursue whatever Vision the Universe might reveal to you. Honesty builds a degree of integrity that stands you in good stead in all the worlds.

EXERCISE: TURNING LEAVES

☆ Start in your sacred space or take yourself to a quiet place in the Otherworld where you can sit beside, or in, a drift of fallen leaves. Take time to think about the leaves, rest your thoughts on them, see them as fragments of your past. This mound of leaves is also a mound of memories.

☆ As you feel ready, slide a hand into the mound and lift out a leaf, turning it over to see an image of your past captured thereon. This may be a word, a picture, or even an experience played back like a video framed by the shape of the leaf. Watch the image, remind yourself of the feelings it held, look at what you did and why. Do not judge yourself, simply observe. Recognise what has gone before. Accept what you have done. Return the leaf to the pile and lift another.

☆ Initially, let your leaf images come at random. Don't try to go through your life in chronological order. Trust your instinct to lift a leaf that you are ready to see (although that may not always be an entertaining experience). With practice, however, you might choose to go looking for experiences that relate to a particular issue and your leaves can become a source of advice on personal patterns and contexts for current behaviours.

☆ Sometimes, people have a particular place where memory vaults are stored. A cave strewn with the leaves of your past might be a secret and private place that only you can visit, another haven within the Otherworld like your sacred space. Or people may simply reach out a hand on a windy day and catch a leaf blowing past to see what memory is waiting to come out.

☆ When you tire of looking, carefully draw your thoughts back from the leaves so that you walk away from a pile of leaves waiting for wind, rain and worms to compost them, not from a collection of your memories.

Variations

Instead of using leaves and woodland, you might care to visit a library and lift the book of your life from the shelves, or go to a cave where your life is painted along the walls. Whatever form you use, find something that can reveal things at random: a book that falls open where it will, a candle that lights up only one part of the cave at a time.

Using the Information

At the conclusion of the session, rather than trying to remember all the details you may have seen, it is often more valuable to feel the emotions that you have worked with and the patterns that recur in your life. Do you see a lot of anger? Fear? Joy? Do you see patterns of possessiveness in friendship? Fixations upon lists? Recognising patterns is the beginning of owning them rather than being owned by them. In future, you may start to identify familiar behaviours in your life – 'Ah, I'm doing *that* again, am I?' – and with this you can start to make your own choices about what you do.

Try writing down the feelings that come with the memories, or draw images that capture your responses. Useful and simple poems can come from words spilled on to a page and shifted around: look for rhythm and feel rather than structure and rhyme and use the words to call up feelings and perhaps release them. Write a letter to yourself about yourself, or another to the world about your hopes, intentions and fears. Or dance out the passion of your experiences.

5

Integrity –
Relationships with
Spirits

The world teems with life. Wherever we are, whatever we do, there are other living things near us: plants root in the cracks of the pavement, seeds lodge in the most polished of frontages, ants infiltrate even the most secure of buildings. For a shaman, all these living things hold spirit, are touched by awareness, maybe not as individuals but certainly as collectives. There is a force, a presence, a character that is the thought and voice of the ants, the flowers, or sometimes the individual flower itself. It does not stop with plants and animals. A shaman's experience of awareness can encompass anything. She is just as likely to meet the awareness of stones, a building, or the wind where it rises on the edge of a cliff. Spirit takes shape all around us, and where we have not met spirits it is more than likely because we have not been aware of them than because they are not there at all. For a shaman, all the world is alive and she has to find ways of becoming open to any communication that her world might want to make, or that she needs to have with the world.

From an early stage in their careers, shamans start to build relationships with spirit people. Variously called helpers, servants, power animals, totems or even angels, these spirits work with the shaman as guides through the Otherworld, as defenders from danger, as messengers, or simply as helpful friends to have around. In a world of teeming possibilities, the new shaman has to find the spirits who are interested in working with her. Does she choose them, or do they choose her? What sort of beings might they be? How does the relationship grow? Who is in charge?

In traditional shamanism, the answers to such questions vary from society to society. As ever, there are very few generalisations. Sometimes a particular culture always works with particular spirits, or the shaman is the master of several spirit servants, or goes questing for a spirit guide. In our work, we will assume that the new shaman is stepping out into the Otherworld without the benefit of an established system behind her.

It is dangerous to make generalisations, but you might expect to find spirits who are:

☆ **Ancestors:** the lingering awareness of past members of your family or society. The ancestors represent a store of the accumulated wisdom of a people, a legacy that the current generation can turn to for advice and guidance. A people survived because they did things in certain ways and it is in the interests of the tribe to maintain those survival traits. Easy contact is usually a feature of continuing traditions rather than broken ones. Ancestor relationships nowadays often have to be carefully sought out rather than being expected to be readily available; sometimes, the ancestors we reach for may not approve at all of the lives we lead or the world we live in. Tread very carefully.

☆ **Animals:** the awareness of animals of the land on which you live, or those that have died out in the physical world fairly recently so that while the hills still remember them their spirits can run with us. Sometimes you will meet a spirit that 'belongs' to an individual animal alive in the everyday world, but more often you meet a spirit who represents a number of those animals or the 'Master Spirit'.

☆ **Plants:** plant spirits work along much the same lines as animal spirits, but where animal spirits tend to appear in their animal shape or maybe as humans with obvious animal attributes, plants seem to be much more flexible and you might meet anything from lively trees to very human flower women giving little clue to their floral origins.

☆ **Landscapes or habitats:** spirits who embody the collective awareness of a woodland, a pond, a river system.

☆ **Faeries:** to use the British term for the people who live in the Otherworld but who are not readily identified as spirits of animals, plants or places. Faeries are faeries. They are simply there, without source, explanation or function, and you will learn to accept them as independent beings.

Old Patterns

In traditional systems, a shaman may be expected to work with particular spirits. Some South American tribes send their shamans to find jaguar spirits or tarantulas, while Saami shamans are said to revere reindeer spirits above all others. Alternatively, shamans may draw from a wider circle of helpers with recognised attributes, and the associations formed become ways of identifying the skills of that shaman.

Many native North American people thus revere Bear Shamans as healers, while Elk Shamans have a potent sexual magic, and so on.

If you are working within a traditional system, you will probably meet spirits who 'belong' to that system and who will measure you by its standards. This has its advantages in that there may be references to draw upon – names of spirits to ask for, associating spirits with particular skills, having access to established ways of working. A familiar ritual might bring spirits more quickly to your side, or if you have a specific job to do, you might know which spirit to go looking for. The spirits also know how they work with 'their' shamans, and the whole relationship follows old, established lines.

New Patterns

If you are trying to find a new path into an old world, these relationships have to start at the beginning. There may turn out to be older patterns and ideas that you can work with, but they will wait for later discovery. When we step into the Otherworld, even when we stay within our own sacred spaces, we are stepping into a world as full of life and activity as the everyday one. Here, we are the strangers, however. We are the ones who have to rediscover a world we walked away from and have to remind ourselves of how to behave within it. It is important to bear this in mind, especially in your early days as a shaman. If you encounter problems with spirits, it is probably because you have, perhaps quite liter-ally, stepped on someone's toes. No-one is under any obligation to be nice to you and some of the spirits you meet may feel they have good reason to be angry with you, or thoroughly unpleasant to you. If you meet landscape spirits whose homes are being destroyed, or the badger spirit whose badger children are being gassed or dug or baited, you may have to talk very fast to avoid being bitten yourself. Real malice is rare, however, although many of the people you may encounter are wild, fierce and independent and should be approached with care, if at all. This is not a world where you can go skipping blithely through a field of flowers without asking permission. That eases with time. As you settle into being a part of the Otherworld you learn, almost instinctively, what you can do and when you need to tread with more care.

Establishing and working in a sacred space is a bit like holding up a neon sign saying 'something new here!', and you can expect the Otherworld's inhabitants to come and check you out in their own ways. Some will look in with mild curiosity, others may be attracted to you as a kindred spirit. Tread with care; don't rush to embrace the first thing that steps up to say 'hello' – it might be a porcupine.

There is an image I use to represent these relationships that bears repeating. Think of your encounters with the spirits of the Otherworld in the same way as you would meeting people in your everyday life. There are folk you will meet only briefly, your lives barely touching: the person next to you in a queue, the person whose shopping you catch as it falls. Other people move within your circle of acquaintances: neighbours on your street, people from the next office – you recognise them, you might stop for a brief chat, or see them at occasional parties. Then there are friends: those groups of people who you are closest to – not necessarily people you spend a lot of time with, but those who understand you, who you would choose to spend time with – people who are comfortable together, who can laugh, be lively and relax together with equal ease. And finally, rarely, there is that person who walks straight into your heart, who slides past all your defences and fits snugly into your innermost places: the soulmate, the totem, the companion whose absence from your life, once found, seems inconceivable.

The first spirit who drops in to look you over might prove to be your totem or they might just have been passing by. Be careful before you go offering your heart on a plate to the first stranger you meet.

Gradually, a spirit family will grow around you: a collection of spirits who, for one reason or another, choose to spend time with you. Some may be there for years, others may drop in now and then, others may be around only for as long as you need them or they need you, and still others, usually just one, slips right inside and becomes a part of you. Terms are always difficult at these times as different words mean different things to people, but for me a 'totem' is the last of these spirits – the one who is a part of you before you ever met and with whom you are greater than either is on their own. All the others are 'the family'; I might call them 'power animals' or even 'guides' but 'family' describes the relationships more accurately.

Honesty and Integrity

In the Otherworld, spirits will work with you because they have chosen to do so, because they respect, trust, and maybe even love you. All that is earned. The spirits are watchful and wary and you will earn their trust and respect by what you do and how you do it more than by the nice words you use. Double standards are instantly damning, but when you act you must do so because it is the right thing for you to do, not because there might be someone watching. That is a measure of your honesty with yourself and becomes the spirits' way of knowing that the integrity you bring to your relationships with them comes from your heart rather than from some political calculation on your part.

When looking at you, if the spirits see ease and joy in life, a readiness for adventure and the guts to say 'I am Me Myself, so push off!' when necessary, they are much more likely to meet you as a possible friend than as a possible meal. It is all right to be afraid and to acknowledge your fear. You gain more respect if you can face a dribbling member of the Unseelie Court (the 'Bad Faeries' of Scottish folklore) and say 'Yes, you scare me helpless. But I am still not going to run away', than if you stand full of bluster and in denial of your feelings.

Patience

Some spirits (including yourself) will be much more wary than others. Memories persist of magicians summoning and binding spirits, of exorcisms and servitude that have left a legacy of suspicion of all things human. So move gently and be prepared to take hold of your courage and make the first move, the one that leaves you exposed and vulnerable, when the moment feels right. You may have quite a wait before a watcher decides whether to show itself or not, but your patience could be part of its measure of you, so do not march out and demand a result.

When you do finally see your visitor, don't run away shrieking or shrug with disappointment because a mouse turned up when you were expecting a wolf. The person who slithers out of the undergrowth will almost certainly not be who you were expecting, but that is probably all to the good as you will not approach them with lots of preconceptions. I once spent a long time listening to a wild boar getting closer, snuffling and snorting. Boars are a family emblem, dramatic, hairy, goddess animals. And then a lynx stepped smiling into my circle and confused me completely . . . but we have been together ever since.

In the everyday imagery and in the magic of most cultures, certain animals and plants will be seen as examples of particular qualities. In Britain, foxes are cunning, oaks are majestic, sheep stupid, lions brave and noble, magpies thieves, and so on. If you are shaping new relationships, try not to label the spirits you meet. Learn from your relationship with the spirit rather than from your society's stereotyping or someone else's categorisation in a book. It is more exciting this way, full of laughter and wonder. You may find that you can learn about bravery from a mouse, grace from a sheep and excitement from a pine sapling.

Some of the old associations do still hold, however, and sometimes spirits do prove true to 'type'. Fox and crow spirits are often tricksters and certainly British crows also move with the presence of the fierce, dark crow goddess behind them and they are tricky, wise and dangerous all at once. Wolf spirits are still seen as powerful and wise, deer often embody the whole force of life of western European woodlands as do the various green men and jack-in-the-greens who turn up now and then. On the whole, however, it is probably safer to step out with a relaxed attitude and explore the relationships that form with whoever chooses to turn up.

Becoming Friends

Do not get lost or swamped by your new friends; always remember that 'I am Me Myself'. You can set limits: of when you can come out to play and how often, of their arrival in the physical world, of what you are prepared to do and how far you will go. Spirits can push you, often asking things of you before you feel you are ready. In time, you will come to trust their measure of you, and when they feel you are ready to be eaten or hunted, to heal or to teach, maybe you will be ready to believe them.

Enjoy getting to know a new friend or friends. Some of those friendships may be transient, others may last for a life-time. Watch your own patterns of behaviour; remember your honesty, do not try to own these people, or control them, but respect them as friends and colleagues, as a family of people with different skills, perceptions, ways of being, seeing and dreaming, who stay together because it is a good thing to do.

The bonds that hold a spirit family together run very deep and the relationships come to lie at the heart of a shaman's power. Your family becomes part of your inspiration, your strength and your love. Enjoy them.

EXERCISE: DEVELOPING RELATIONSHIPS

When you have met a spirit, find ways of working together. You might:

☆ Be gentle with each other.

☆ Rest yourself for a while inside your spirit friend (easier done than described) and see the world through their eyes.

☆ Dance together as partners or slide in and out of each other again so that sometimes you may be dancing hand in paw with a badger, then dancing as a badger woman, and then back again.

☆ Move together through the Otherworld in silence and stealth. What secrets do you discover?

☆ Draw patterns in sand (over there) or on paper (back here), colours and shapes that describe the two of you, swirls, lines, spirals, dots, footprints, eyes, feathers — perhaps as designs for embroidery or face painting.

☆ Find the bounds of the relationship — are there things you should or should not do: eat the flesh of your friend? Plant its seeds? Scrub clean the wells that it celebrates?

Treat this as a new friendship. Behave towards your spirit as you would like it to behave toward you. Experiment.

EXERCISE: BRINGING THINGS DOWN TO EARTH

Back in the everyday world, you can draw upon the inspiration of Otherworld sessions to create:

☆ A spirit dance — a simple set of steps that capture the essence of the movement and emotion of your spirit friend. This might be a dance to use for yourself, to teach to human friends, or to use with a working group of people to support you as you and your spirit work together in the centre of their dancing ring.

☆ A spirit song. Take some scribbled words, cut them up and jiggle them around. Look for rhythm and repeating sounds, a flow, a pattern that can be easily learned so that you can sing together, spirit and shaman side by side.

☆ 'Power objects' – either drawn, painted, sewn or carved, and inspired by Otherworld experiences.

These become tools to work with, physical hands that help your spirit reach out into the physical.

Get Dirty

Find ways of supporting your spirit friends in the everyday world. If you are friends with plant or animal spirits, you might care for their physical forms by supporting a relevant conservation organisation, feeding the ducks in the park, planting seeds or protecting trees. Similar activities unfold with all spirits: they know which things give them support and joy – the things that perhaps our ancestors used to do. This is not necessarily because they got special benefits from doing them but because they were good or neighbourly things to do. Clean out a holy well. Pick up litter. Value the little woodland in a local park. Scrub the feet of a statue. Stroke the carvings on old buildings because you recognise the beauty of them.

Love the world – it is probably the greatest gift you can give your family.

6

Vision

At some point in his training, every apprentice shaman must go 'on the hill', out into the wide, wild world and hope that that world will vouchsafe him a Vision, will acknowledge him as a shaman and show him the path to his own personal power. For a shaman, the Vision that comes spinning out of the darkness and swallows him in a blizzard of images and experiences is one of the key moments of his life.

Most shamanic traditions do not have communal initiation rituals as you might find in other magical or religious traditions. There will be threshold events for the apprentice shaman – the first time he works with his community in the presence of his teacher, the first time he works alone, the first time he gets it completely wrong – there may be a formal welcoming into the community as a shaman, but there are rarely rituals that install him in his shamanic power. Those ceremonies happen for him alone on a hill before the singing presence of all the world. Sometimes, shamans-to-be receive their guiding Visions during serious illness or some other near-death experience, but for the person training to become a shaman, a Visionquest ceremony, or its equivalent, could be planned. A Visionquest is a planned withdrawal from everyday life: a time of solitude and reflection where the shaman humbles himself before the Infinite and prays for a Vision, a revelation, that will confirm him on the path that he is following. The Vision he receives might also reveal ceremonies for his use, a powersong, a personal name and spirit companions if he does not have any already. But the heart of it all is the Vision.

The Eye of the Storm

In our image of the double spiral, Vision lies at the centre of the spiral – a moment of dynamic balance, a stillness where both inward and outward movements are poised, an end, a beginning, the eye of the storm. When the shaman sets out hoping for a Vision, he lays aside all his defences, all the layers of mystery, arrogance and comedy that we shelter behind, and he stands alone and exposed before the world. Even his spirit family will probably have removed themselves and be waiting elsewhere. In some ways this is as much a test for them as it is for him; they have gone along with him, they believe in his abilities, and now they will see if their faith has been justified. Will the shaman have enough honesty to be humble, enough courage to be helpless, enough humility to wonder at the hugeness of the world? The Native American Lakota/Sioux Visionquest ceremony is called *Hanblecheyapi*, which is usually translated as 'crying for a Vision'. The shaman stands humble before the Infinite. There is no demand or expectation of success, only stillness and hope within the heart. Vision finally comes as a moment of clear communication between the shaman, his innermost self, his spirit, the world, the Infinite, and the Web as a whole.

Vision is not a casual divination, a chance casting of the

runes or the Tarot, but a time of deep stillness and awe-inspiring connection with the Infinite. Vision on this scale may only happen once in a lifetime or it may come more often, but there is a huge difference between 'visions', things seen or experienced here and there in the everyday and in the Otherworlds, and Vision. In Vision, the world speaks to you, through spirits or gods or simply as itself out of the stretching darkness of the night; in Vision, the shaman perceives the path that his spirit is trying to follow, the life his spirit is trying to lead, a way along the Web that will allow him to move in harmony with the world and to promote harmony in the people he works with.

Images

Vision rarely reveals finite or definite images. Sometimes it reveals rituals that must be performed, but Vision is more likely to show images than the overall shape of things. The following descriptions of visions are taken from conversations with modern shamans:

☆ Hand in hand with a stranger, a sense of caring, *I'm in his heart, feeling his pain.*

☆ Waves on a shore, seaweed swaying, *I move with grace, I flow, like seaweed, I shape myself around obstacles, but I am rock-fast, glued on to the stone.*

☆ White horse running free over a rising field, *I am the horse, I am moving, and with the drumming of heart and feet, I carry, support and move on.*

☆ Dancing alone in deep forest and dancing in company on a

village green, I am jack-in-the green, I am the dancing season, cycles returned and renewed, remorseless as death but full of life.

From the images of Vision, the shaman finds a sense of direction: he is a maker, a builder, a healer, a shaper, a talker, a teacher. Visions can be frustratingly vague. You can feel the passion of it, the rightness of what you experienced, but what does it mean? Sometimes an experienced teacher can help, while at other times, you have to trust the Vision itself, relax and invite the Vision to move through your everyday life and see what changes come.

You are unlikely to come out of a Visionquest with a neat list saying, 'My Vision is *this*, so I have to do *that* and *that* and *that*.' Vision reveals a personal pattern; it is not some fixed destiny or fate. How you 'live your Vision', how you bring its principles into action in your everyday and Otherworld work is up to you. Vision may suggest that you are a one-to-one healer, but you could express that in any number of ways. You might want to be an all-singing, all-dancing, rattles and drums shamanic soul-retrieval wonder-worker. Or you might work best as a doctor, a nurse, a herbalist, a therapist . . . when your actions come from your Vision, they are all worthy of respect, and you should respect yourself for following the Vision rather than the self-aggrandisement that might have made a more obviously shamanic path of action appealing.

A Sense of Purpose

Anyone can ask for a Vision. It is not the exclusive right of a 'shaman'. Among the Lakota people, it was expected that all young people should seek a Vision when they stood on the threshold of adulthood. this was a rite of passage that recognised the step from childhood into their independent adult lives. The Vision received could be expected to reveal an adult name, totem or other personal power symbols, and a purpose for their lives, such as warriors, hunters, horse-tamers, home-makers. The tribal shaman worked with the young person to prepare them for their ceremony and was the first person they met when they returned from their Visionquest; someone who would listen and help interpret the Vision.

Visions are not always straightforward. They should not be seen simply as confirmations of existing ambitions. You can expect a Vision to throw you sideways in your life. Among the Lakota, people were expected to live out the pattern revealed in their Vision regardless of its consequences. The community would support the men who then lived as women, or the women who broke the mould and became warriors, or the *heyokas*, the backwards people, whose lives are spent doing everything the wrong way round. Respect was earned by living your Vision, not by conforming meekly to a cultural norm.

In Western cultures, we have largely lost that time of withdrawal and communion that allows revelation. Even our rites of passage have dwindled, and now only the bawdy, raucous tail-end survives as 18th or 21st birthday parties and the like. Some modern shamans are now facilitating the return of rites of passage (regardless of age) and creating opportunities for individuals to 'go on the hill' and listen to the voice of the world speaking with their self.

Visionquests and Vigils

A Western equivalent of *Hanblecheyapi* might be found in the Vigil of the medieval squire on the eve of his knighthood. He would spend that last night of youth, kneeling before the cross hilt of his sword before the altar of a chapel, praying for strength and guidance. It was a time of silence and contemplation, a chance for fears to be acknowledged, hopes explored and somewhere in the long, cold darkness, for the touch of the bright hand of the Lord to bless the new warrior.

Whether the quest for Vision takes place on a *Hanblecheyapi* hilltop or in a squire's chapel, the event of glory and revelation seems to remain the same. Perhaps Vigil can be distinguished from Vision in that it might take place indoors, but this is a pedantic distinction. An indoor Vigil is as valid as the outdoor Visionquest. It is also not necessarily an easier option, particularly if the shaman is working in a cold, stone building, and may often prove a more 'haunted' occasion. Vigils call for old buildings, places made of stone and heavy with the weight of their years, places of presence and atmosphere. The shaman might choose to spend his Visionquest there among the stones, and in the night the memories of all the lives lived in that place might come crowding around him. While Vision as described here reveals the shaman to the world, with Vigil the shaman possibly opens himself up even more directly to his human ancestry.

So, Vision lies at the heart of a shaman's work. While so much of that work is for others, Vision is very personal. It is the guidance for the shaman alone, the strength and support that lies at the centre of the double spiral. Vision provides a standard to measure things against: does this action run with the path of Vision or cut across it? If I do this do I betray my Vision?

Fate or Guidance?

Vision does not hold tyrannical rule over a shaman's life, trapping him within rigid walls of action. With Vision, the shaman learns to sense the 'rightness' of actions, like finding the path home in the dark. That 'rightness' helps him sense appropriate actions, to feel his way into the lives of his people and find the paths that will take them safely home, where home might be health, release from fear or a life moving in harmony with the world.

Of course, sometimes you will get it wrong. Or you will forget and go dashing off after something colourful and glamorous, or get swamped by everyday things – and feel that you are losing your Vision in the washing-up, the bank statements and keeping a roof over your head. It remains, however, hidden under everything else and will always return. Once you have let yourself see your Vision and have acknowledged it, it becomes hard to live successfully against it. If you are lost, you can stop and let the river find you and pick you up. If you try to avoid Vision, to block or deny it, like a river always returning to the easiest course down a valley, it will erode or destroy whatever obstructs its path. Those obstacles could easily include yourself as you try to do other things, or look for an easy life, or even an everyday life. You should only go looking for Vision if you are prepared to follow the Vision that speaks to you.

All the above applies to some extent to any life with Vision, whether you see yourself as a shaman or not. For a shaman, Vision does become binding – not constricting, but bonding. If you are a shaman, and you are pursuing Vision through your work and your life, then you should, hopefully, gradually stop doing inappropriate things – foolish things; and, we would hope, the completely stupid things. Being a shaman is not a selfish process. If you are a shaman and have offered yourself in service to the world, the service will be shaped by Vision, by your heart speaking to you. Working against your Vision trips you up; denying your Vision is to invite a slap in the face. We come back again to the honesty of the inward spiral. You cannot live within your Vision only when it suits you. Your whole life becomes bound up with following your Vision.

EXERCISE: VISIONQUEST

In a traditional Visionquest, a shaman may encounter a whole range of experiences; there may be moments of revelation, the shock of dismemberment, the finding of a powersong and singing it to the world. Although this chapter and the following exercise concentrate on the 'revelation' part of the experience, you may find yourself sliding from one component to another during your own Vision without any obvious transition points. Often the different elements only become clear upon reflection; at the time you are so immersed in it all that you go wherever the vision takes you.

Afterwards, you might look for the following factors:

☆ **Dismemberment:** being taken apart, or even eaten, by spirits to release your spirit from its need to hold on to a human shape.

☆ **Revelation:** the Vision of this chapter.

☆ **Powersong or dance:** the words and movement that become your personal gateway to the Otherworld.

☆ **Facing the world:** after revelation, you may find yourself still standing facing the night, with all the world watching you, not now as an individual seeking purpose, but as a shaman they might choose to work

with: 'What can you do?', 'Why should we notice you?'
Sing your powersong, dance your dance.

☆ **Bringing the power home:** meeting your mentor
or helper and singing your song to them; bringing what
you have seen or learned into the everyday world;
prove to all of us that you can do it.

In the Otherworld you can choose the shape you wear. You
are spirit, the living energy of the Web and you can dream
the body you wear. In the Otherworld body shape describes
you but it does not define you. You are free.

EXERCISE: PLANNING A VISIONQUEST

☆ **When am I ready?** When you feel you are ready,
or when your spirit family or your mentor feel you are.
Sometimes, you can feel the need, like an urgency or a
pressure building and know that the time is right. Or
you may go through all the activities and preparations
and find that the night stays quiet. If so, wait, practise
your work and try again.

☆ **Vision or Vigil?** Where should the quest happen?
Key factors here are isolation and atmosphere. You
need to find a site where you will be left undisturbed
for at least 12 hours (usually at night), a site that is in
some way special for you. Within that place, you may
move around when you begin your ceremony to find
the ideal spot for you at this time. A Visionquest might
be based on a hilltop, in a cave, by a lakeside or in a
deep woodland glade. Visionquest might become Vigil
if you choose to work within walls, but do not settle for

the spare room or a neighbour's attic! Look for a place with a sense of presence and the weight of years.

Preparations

☆ **Magical:** in the build-up to your quest, work to explore stillness, meditate, sing and dance. Look after yourself and come to the ceremony with a clear head. Avoid alcohol or other drugs for the days beforehand; eat simple food; prepare a bundle.

☆ **Practical:** be thorough and sensible. Make sure someone knows where you are going and when you should be back. Ideally arrange for someone to drop you off and pick you up again, hopefully a person you can talk to about the whole experience. Do not take a lot of equipment with you, but do have warm and waterproof clothing, a tarpaulin and a blanket, candles, matches, flask, water and a first-aid kit. You could always have an emergency box back at your meeting point with food, a torch and a mobile phone.

☆ **How long?:** the Lakota traditionally took four days and four nights but this takes a lot of building up to. Even 12 hours is often quite daunting for a first time. Do not eat during this time if you can: sip water or maybe even take some tea and chocolate for energy, but do not plan cheerful packed lunches and midnight feasts.

During the Quest

☆ Stay awake!

☆ Start and end with an offering – incense, a dance, a token tied to a tree.

☆ Sing or dance.

☆ Rattle and stamp.

☆ Take time to be still.

☆ Expect lots of distractions, reasons to leave, decisions that it is all over now.

☆ Watch.

☆ Listen.

☆ Notice the little things.

☆ Stay awake!

7

Humility – Approaching the Gods

The experience of Vision is both inspiring and humbling. Alone before the Infinite, the shaman appreciates the immensity of it all, the wonder of being part of this great shining world, this Wakan-Tanka, this Great Mystery. The marvel of it wakes our humility. For all a shaman's strength and experience, she sees that she is as nothing before the world, but that even so she is as much a part of this whole, huge Web of life as anything else, with as much right to be there as anything else. A shaman's humility is not based on being subdued or intimidated by another's power but on being overwhelmed by wonder.

The Gods of the Shamans

With shamanic traditions scattered all across the world and manifesting in a myriad of forms, there is no conformity in the deities that shamans address. There is no generally recognised shamanic god or goddess. For some there is the

Infinite, a nameless, faceless force, while Black Elk's Wakan-Tanka, the Great Mystery, is given many names. For yet other cultures, the Infinite takes on a more personal form as spirits, similar to the familiar spirits of the Otherworld but older and greater. We might be tempted to call them 'gods' but they are not 'worshipped' as such. Like the Dreamtime ancestors of the native Australians, they are our forefathers, not necessarily human but the spirits we derived from. The shaman can reach out to them, talk to them, but rarely worships them.

There are also 'gods' who are different from the spirits, identified as greater, sometimes older, more powerful, worthy of deeper respect than everyday and Otherworld people, who hold the ultimate power over the life and death of those various peoples. Then, even more confusingly, we might meet spirits in our everyday lives who behave like any other spirit, but who are often tricksters and troublemakers. Yet these mischief-makers are also, or have been, major creator spirits, 'gods' in any other language.

In shamanic cultures the connection between a people and their most powerful beings is often a direct one. Sometimes the shaman is the channel by which a god communicates with his people, at other times any member of the community may approach the Great Mystery or find that the Dreamtime ancestor of her totem group within the clan is speaking to her.

It is difficult to discover just how a shamanic culture perceives its gods, however. It may be that that culture does not actually recognise greater beings, misunderstands an interviewer's expectation of 'supreme beings' (too often a measure of 'civilisation' among early researchers), is wary of revealing these most personal of things to outsiders, or feels that these are things that are simply not spoken about. They are sacred, maybe too sacred to be easily expressed.

Shamans work with the gods of the culture they belong to, or sometimes with 'foreign' gods who have arrived in the shaman's work and expect to be noticed. For a modern shaman, the gods watching may be those of the system you are working with: the Creator Spirits of Medicine Wheel teachings, perhaps, or the Loa of West African and Caribbean traditions, or you may have no particular connection with the gods you might meet.

But meet them you surely will. Like so much else in a shaman's world, you need to work with the realisation that there is something *out there*. Shamanism, is not a religion as such: it does not advocate a specific set of teachings about the worship of a particuar deity. But the shaman knows that there are beings out there who are much more powerful than she is, more powerful than the spirits who are her friends, beings who speak perhaps for whole areas of the Web at a time, or may even speak for the whole Web.

If we, as individuals, are points on the Web, following our own threads and touching others, and if the spirits we work with are other individual points, or even the collective awareness of a small group of points (a landscape spirit who speaks for a woodland, an animal spirit representing the local population of foxes), the gods can be seen as the consciousness of a large area of the Web – all of a river, a land, the sky, the sea, all animals, the planet or a galaxy. This suggests a hierarchy, perhaps: a layered pantheon of greater and lesser deities, maybe with a 'top' god or goddess. And behold! We have just designed ourselves an Olympus with Zeus and Hera, or God, the archangels and all the company of cherubim and seraphim.

Of course, it rarely works in such an organised way. A shaman's relationship with a deity is as personal as all the other aspects of her work. There is rarely any intermediary:

no priest to stand between person and deity and interpret Divine wishes. When a shaman's gods want her to do something, they tend to tell her personally. A shaman's gods are beings who she meets as people: not as impersonal embodiments of anything, but as the people who are at the back of her power, the root of her life, the overall force of the living, unfolding Web. Every shaman finds her own relationship with those beings: with one or two of them or with a whole pantheon. The number of gods you work with is not a measure of your success: you do not set off to choose the ones you fancy, you work with those who turn up and shout at you. A shaman's gods are 'Those Who Watch' and when they are ready, they will walk into your life and then you will know. Their presence is unmistakable and their arrival is as likely to have you hiding under the bed or running shrieking down the street as falling to your knees in religious rapture.

When they come walking into your life, everything is liable to change. The shaman in her training will realise that very little in her world is fixed. Most things are fluid, negotiable even. Relationships evolve. The paths to awareness and power are not mapped, solid roads, but winding trails that we pick for ourselves through the trees. The Otherworld shapes itself around our images, the dreams we offer it until we are sensitive enough to experience it through its own dreams. But the gods are something else altogether. The faces of the Infinite, they are out there, watching, waiting, choosing their moment (rather than our moment) to come striding into our lives.

Meeting the Gods

The gods will be who they choose to be. As the consciousness of the Web, the gods see wider reaches of the pattern than anyone else. They see where we have grown from and further ahead into the patterns we are weaving. They protect the whole and tend the growing of the whole. When they talk to us, they find the forms that they are familiar with and that we might recognise. They give themselves faces so that there is someone to talk to rather than leaving us shouting into the emptiness of space (although that happens sometimes too).

If you are working within a particular system, the chances are that you will meet the gods of that system, for example Odin and the Aesir and Vanir of the Nordic worlds, or sea-born Sedna from Inuit tales. This is by no means certain, however. In a system or out of it, if you are working with the land you live upon, you can expect almost anyone from that land's store of myths, peoples and landscapes to come visiting. In Britain, we might meet the Dagda or the Morrigan from Celtic worlds, or Freya from our Nordic past, while a mixed British folk tradition might turn up Herne, Wotan, or Black Annis, or anyone else drawn from the rich variety of peoples and cultures that have populated these islands. Elsewhere, you might meet the gods of your blood: Lugh or Brigid of Celtic ancestry may appear, changed by the land you now live in and thus decked in the flowers of your Australian or American home rather than those of her ancestral one.

Relationships with the Gods

We are shamans. We live in a world that changes. And just as with our other spirit companions, we learn not to analyse our gods. We do not set out with a firm intention of working only with this one or that one and dismiss any that do not conform to our standards. Most modern shamans recognise four patterns of relationshps with deity:

(1) Approaching a faceless but usually compassionate Infinite – the Great Mystery, the consciousness of everything, a force that manifests in many ways but rarely becomes an individual named 'god'.

(2) Working with a variable pantheon of mixed deities with no particular allegiance to any one of them.

(3) Bonding with one or two distinct beings who might take different shapes at different times but who are clearly all aspects of the same personality; a moon goddess with many faces, a nature god who changes with the seasons.

(4) No 'gods' as such, but a recognition of some spirits as more powerful than others, approached more seldom, and seen as more influential.

It might be said that these patterns are one and the same: all gods are aspects of the Infinite, all gods change to suit themselves, all gods are illusions, shapes designed to make the Universe human and accessible. And so they might be. A shaman's gods are often even trickier than she is and are quite capable of bursting any bubbles of illusion she is cultivating about them. They can remind her that they are but illusions and dreams, faces plucked from anywhere, and affirm the power of their personal existence all in the same breath. Yet again there are no rules here: the shaman has to find out how she relates to the deities that are interested in her and if that feels right, to stick with it, however disturbing and frightening.

The apprentice shaman needs to use her instincts, trust her spirits and listen to the world. Analysing gods is liable to be seen as presumptuous or contemptuous and dealt with accordingly. But one day, when you are working, or walking, or having a cup of tea, you might feel a gaze upon you and the next time you go to the Otherworld perhaps someone else will be there, too; someone to whom all spaces are sacred and so can walk where She will – into your most guarded of sacred spaces, who might cradle you, cuddle you, stamp on you and drag you through stones. The 'test' for yourself is the awe of Her presence. She fills the world, because She is the world, the Web, the Infinite. Nevertheless, here She is, focused down into a single form, a face to talk to.

Often, modern shamans find that they form relationships with one or two gods. As with other spirit relationships, these can be powerful and very emotional. Like totems and spirit families, the gods you work most closely with are part of what makes you whole. 'Ownership' may seem a dangerous word, but as a shaman you work to serve the world, and with gods as the faces and voices of that world, you do become their servant. Not that this is a relationship of acquiescence; shamans often argue with everything, but your gods are among the very few beings who have the authority to expect a shaman to do as they request.

The shaman stands in this world and the Otherworld. She moves between the two, her spirit family beside her, her community around her. Beneath her feet is the land, feeding her and shaping her flesh, and behind her stand the gods, encompassing mystery and passion to thrill the blood and release her from the world, carrying her beyond the edges of the Otherworld and into the spaces between all the worlds. The domain of the Great Mystery stretches from the depths of the earth to the farthest reaches of the stars. The shaman's gods are the voice of the mystery in her life.

Contacting the Gods

You cannot do exercises as such to bring you closer to the gods. When they are ready to approach you they will,

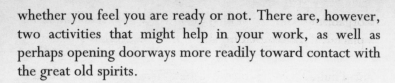

whether you feel you are ready or not. There are, however, two activities that might help in your work, as well as perhaps opening doorways more readily toward contact with the great old spirits.

EXERCISE: COMMUNION

☆ Value your times of stillness. Enter the Otherworld, relax and be still. Try not to do anything else – no personal examinations or complicated powersongs. Appreciate the stillness. Go through the stillness regime from the Touching Stillness exercise in Chapter 1 and open your eyes now in both worlds. Perhaps make an offering of smoke or flame (incense or a single candle). Watch that action in both worlds. Then be still.

☆ Sometimes these quiet times will be solitary and peaceful. At others, you may find that your spirit family joins you without any need for songs or rattles, and you share that time together. And, just occasionally, the breath of something else will touch you. Often this is a time when you will feel the next step you should take – *return here in the darkness, follow the path through the trees to the stones . . .*

☆ With communion you are saying that you are ready, willing and, hopefully, able to meet some of the greater spirits of the Otherworld.

EXERCISE: MAKING SHRINES

Shamans tends to accumulate things: the fetishes we make, odd stones, bones and cuddly animals that we find and that feel as though they want to be with us for a while. You can discipline this accumulation by organising some of your finds into shrines. A shrine is a place for contemplation and reflection around a theme.

☆ Find a space, probably a flat surface (but you could work with a box on a wall or even decorate the frame of a mirrow or a picture). You might plan a long-term shrine or perhaps a seasonal or a short celebratory, midsummer or wedding shrine.

☆ From your assorted finds, select things that reflect your chosen theme. You might also make a new artefact or stalk things of particular relevance. It is important to make an effort. Show commitment in the planning and assembling of your shrine and dedication in maintaining it.

☆ Usually, a shrine will include a place for offerings (a small bowl for incense or a cup for wine) and a point of concentration (a candle on its own or in front of a statuette, or a bowl of water reflecting a flame).

☆ Once it is assembled, try to use your shrine on a regular basis. Meditate, practise communion in front of it, say a charm or a prayer, or dedicate an offering at the shrine. If we are cooking a special meal in my house, tokens of the food and drink are left on the household shrine. Contact might be fleeting, a moment of attunement to start the day, perhaps, or you might follow a whole Otherworld journey while seated in front of it.

8

The Dreaming Land

The Land holds everything together. In traditional shamanic societies the importance of the Land as provider, protector and destroyer is recognised. The Land gives firewood, shelter, food and water, and acting against the law of the land might bring floods, storms, dangerous animals or the demons that cause disease. All the concepts discussed in previous chapters come together in the work of a shaman holding his people and the Land in harmony.

Much of a shaman's work is very active: seeking advice, healing people, travelling among the spirits and finding paths, and some of the deeper and more subtle consequences of a shamanic life can be lost under the more obvious roles of healer, speaker and patterner. An awareness of and relationship with the Land lies beneath everything the shaman does, behind the trance work, the inspiring deities, and the talk of Webs and wheels. Shamanism seems to have evolved as a way of developing and expressing the relationship between a people and the land they lived upon. Even now, that relationship remains at the root of a shaman's work. It must not be forgotten. Deeper than trance visits to the Otherworld, deeper than talk of gods or demons, the Land lies at the root of everything. The Land is the Web made physical. All those relationships we speak of, the delicate ones we track between people and spirits, are nothing without the Land. In today's technological world, it is all too easy to forget that our lives depend upon the Land we walk on. It seems as if it has always been there, and will always be there. It seems to demand nothing of us and we so easily take it for granted. But the Land is life, *our* life. We ignore it, abuse it and destroy it at our peril, for even more than the air we breathe, the water we drink and the food we eat, it is the stuff of our flesh. Our blood, bones and bodies are made of the earth we walk over.

To traditional shamans that relationship is very clear and its potency never forgotten. Where talk of 'webs' and similar patterns may seem an intellectual abstraction, a useful way of describing the patterns of life, the Land reminds us of the reality of those connections, the patterns of living and dying. Here the remorseless flow of life swallows people in the freezing cold of a northern winter or the burning heat of an African desert, and in the wondrous strength of purpose that brings the migrating herds back to the north at the end of the cold or bursts the desert into bloom after sudden rain. Our relationship with the Land is bigger than almost anything else: the Land holds the people, the spirits and the gods in its compassionate and death-dealing hand and as the pathfinder for his people, the shaman finds ways to maintain and strengthen this relationship and to celebrate and strengthen the Land that is life.

The Need to Reconnect

In Western society, we have long seen ourselves as safely divorced from the apparent vagaries of a life dependent upon the 'goodwill' of our environment, but we are at last realising that that 'safety' was an illusion and that we are as vulnerable, albeit in different ways, as our ancestors. Storms still batter us, roads flood, houses are destroyed, new diseases evolve, changing as fast as new wonder-drugs are produced, and our own chemicals come back to haunt us, working their way through the intricate patterns of the Web to poison our children, hit sperm counts, undermine our immune systems, and perhaps even infiltrate our genetic make-up.

Perhaps the most important thing the modern shaman can do for people is to help them find a new relationship with their Land. They do not need to live with an awareness of it as a waking world as the shaman does, but to survive we must all have respect and appreciation for the world and a readiness to protect its integrity, the clarity of its waters, the diversity of its life.

Celebrate Where You Live

You might not live where you would ideally like to live. You might dream of a wild coastline and the mist on the hills or long for life on a whole other continent while you live in a noisy housing estate or some pocket of suburban tedium. But where you live is your Land for now and you need to find ways of relating to that place rather than to a dream of where you think you want to be. If you eventually reach that wonderful haven, then you can start the connections all over again, but for now you are here and this is where you must shape your cycles of people and Land.

As with so much else in the shaman's training, this is not a highly organised sequence of investigations and deliberations. To start, the shaman needs to become open to the Land beneath his feet, to slip into the Otherworld and simply go exploring. He does not enter with a fixed goal, but sets out to walk and wander and marvel at where those wanderings take him and at what he meets along the way. This may, in time, give him ideas as to what he should do for the Land where he lives.

When we start touching the Land, as with the gods, we move in a world that operates on a completely different scale from the one we are used to. We may already have met spirits of places: a stream, pond or well, or the goddess who holds a river from spring to mouth, and all of these may speak to us more or less as living aspects of the Land. But the Land itself . . . a shaman knows that the Land is alive. It is awake and aware. But it is an awareness that spans aeons, where centuries are but moments in a life of mountain-building and the long, slow crumbling of a headland into the sea. This is not an awareness based on living and dying as ours is, but on changing, always forming into new shapes and on a timescale that we can talk about but find it almost impossible to grasp. Against the hills we are very small: all the centuries of this millennium are only a breath in the lives of the hills.

Owners, Stewards or Guardians?

Some people believe that we are the custodians of the Land, others that we are its 'consciousness', and still others that we are the rocks dancing. In the Web, the Land gives physical shape to the pattern of the whole: it is the body of it all, and we are the detail, the thoughts and dreams that provide variety. We are all connected, a part of the Web, and to lose any part affects the rest, diminishing it. The hills may never notice us as individuals, but we are part of the force of transformation, we help keep the Web moving, we are fire, air and water to the Land's stone.

And we do make a difference. Shamans recognise that we have abilities that our fellow animals and the plants do not. The spirits may work their own rituals in the Otherworld but humans offer a way for worlds of spirit and flesh to combine in celebration and ceremony in the physical world. With music, song, dance and focused intention, our ceremonies can empower the Web around us, strengthening people, Land and spirits alike. What this makes of us – leaders, lords, guardians or just the same as everyone else – you will have to decide for yourself. However, while we can sing, dance and shoot things dead, we cannot migrate, for example as the salmon do. We may follow them, predict them and intercept them, but only the salmon themselves can make their epic journey from river to deep sea and back again.

Calendars

In traditional shamanic societies, the relationship between a people and their environment can be followed through their cycles of ceremonies. A tribal calendar might incorporate practical, social and spiritual events: the seasonal movements of nomadic people, clans gathering for large hunts, the harvest of a particular crop, times of trade. It might include the regular and the occasional activities of individuals and families: ploughing, planting, hunting, naming children, marriages, coming of age, death. And then there are ceremonies centred around the relationship of people, spirits and Land: the coming of the rains, sowing the seeds, blessing the harvest, watching for the salmon running in the streams.

The 'shamanic' nature, as we see it, of such events might vary a lot. There may seem to be none at all in some wild horse-racing fair, or there may be a role we identify more with a formal priesthood, presiding at a wedding, perhaps, or there may be the full-scale trance, dance and wild drumming of ceremonies that welcome the spirits back to their homes. To traditional shamans such distinctions are largely irrelevant. Shamans have a job to do for their people and if those people see the shaman as the most appropriate person to lead this event or that ceremony, the shaman will do it. Shamanism is not restricted to obviously 'shamanic' things.

Traditional ceremonies were more than just ways of ensuring next year's harvest. A ceremony is a salute to the Land and the spirits that have provided for a people, but it is also an act of empowerment for those spirits. To return the bones of a salmon to the river where it was caught feeds into that web of connections. A prayer for the returning salmon may be a prayer for the future of a village's food supply, but it is also a prayer on behalf of the bears and otters who also hunt the salmon, a prayer for all the life the salmon brings to the river, for the killer whales waiting in the Sound and for the salmon itself.

A society with totemic relations with the world around them has obligations that go beyond straightforward survival activities. As the spirits who conduct ceremonies in flesh, a shaman, or anyone related through their totem, might find himself called upon to perform ceremonies for the benefit of a particular species. As with a salmon prayer, any ceremony will have repercussions across the area, and in helping his spirit relations a shaman also helps his human community. If the shaman is to continue to work across the worlds, he must listen to and respect the needs of those worlds, and his skills should be available to those who choose to call upon them.

In reaching out to the Land as modern shamans, we need to find that range of activity, looking for old celebrations that have survived, others waiting to be revived or new ones that need to find expression in the everyday world.

The Structure of a Ceremonial Calendar

The ceremonies of a calendar cycle might be communal, involving groups of people of various sizes, or they might be more private, conducted by the shaman or another individual alone or with just one or two people in support, and the spirits and the Land as witnesses. Ceremonies might be regular (seasonal, annual or longer term) or occasional (as needed in the lives of people and the cycles of nature). They might be spontaneous or anticipated, human in origin or inspired by the needs of the spirits or the Land.

Such a calendar of relationships between people and landscape might contain a number of general features:

(1) **Personal links:** activities centred upon relationships with totem or similar spirit people.
(2) **Practical connections:** physical tasks without an obvious ceremonial content.
(3) **Witnessing:** being present at, recognising and maybe celebrating particular events – the first frosts, the first swallows of summer.
(4) **Empowering:** ceremonies that keep the Web moving. These may once have had a much stronger survival value than their modern equivalent, but still serve Land and people.

The ceremonies of a cycle are rarely exclusive or develop with an obvious logical sequence. As discussed above, a 'ceremony' will not always be full of 'shamanic activity'; performed with intention and a love of the place, a physical task may also be an act of respect and celebration.

In your own work, look for this sort of variety: explore ideas that will allow you to work physically and magically, alone and in company. Communal activity does not always need to be organised beforehand; some of the nicest moments can come from passing strangers stopping to lend a hand to people who are dragging handfuls of smelly leaves from the bottom of an old well, or families pausing to light a candle, or weave some token of their own presence into a garland to hang over the water.

The shaman's relationship with the Land becomes his heart-beat; people, spirits and gods give us purpose and inspiration, strength, companionship and support, but the Land lies in the belly and is the life of it all. Touching the awareness of the Land is often as rare as Vision, and is to be valued just as much. Sometime in the Otherworld, you will find that the world changes, that you feel yourself slipping into something else's dream of what the world might be. This is the Dream of the Land, the Otherworld of the hills, the hills thinking of what they might be. It is not an ancestral memory, nor a Golden Age to hark back to – it is the Otherworld of the Land.

To be welcomed into the Dreaming Land is a measure of your acceptance as a shaman. With Vision, you might have heard the world speaking, gained a name, learned a song. But when you slip through the gaps in the Otherworld and into the Dreaming Land you can feel that you are being accepted. We may know in our heads and our hearts that we are all part of the Land, but we only actively become part of it when that awareness has settled so deeply within us that the belonging is no longer questioned. The change is within ourselves. We are giving ourselves to all the world: our people, the spirits, the bones of the Land itself. Then the Land relaxes around us and lets us in, but before you take that step you need to know that there might be no going back.

EXERCISE: CREATING A CALENDAR OF CELEBRATIONS AND CEREMONIES

A shaman needs to recognise and respond to the changing seasons of the year, to his people and their needs and to the needs of his spirit companions. Some of these responses may call for regular celebrations or ceremonies, others may require one-off activities. Chapter 9 describes ways of constructing such ceremonies, while this exercise looks at ways of planning the calendar itself.

New Calendars

☆ Draw three concentric circles on a big sheet of paper and divide them into four season, 12 months, 13 moons or whatever form of annual classificiation you are comfortable with. You will be using the space beyond the outermost circle so do not work right to the edge of your paper.

☆ In the innermost circle: mark your personal landmarks of the changing year – the first swallows in summer, collecting conkers, your birthday, an anniversary, kicking up drifts of dead leaves, stamping on the ice in puddles.

☆ The middle circle represents the calendar of your community – what are the celebrations that are shared by the people around you? Christmas, Easter, Cup Final day, or maybe it is a Western pagan year of Beltane, Lughnasadh, Samhain and Imbolc?

☆ In the outer circle mark the points where the inner and middle circles coincide – what is important in both your personal year and in the community calendar? This is where you can start to create a calendar to work with. You might find that some of the things you want to mark coincide with established celebrations, for example snowdrops, crocuses, Imbolc and Candlemas all occur at about the same time. That could help you plan celebrations that might attract other people and become an exciting community celebration; or your personal observations could slide neatly and quietly into an established event; or you may find that no-one else is interested in 'the day of the first toadspawn', and that might remain as a private ceremony in your calendar.

☆ Before finalising a calendar, talk to your spirit family. Are there features that they would like you to celebrate? With a Toad totem, I mark times of migration to the breeding ponds, toadspawn, metamorphosis and hibernation. This could all be written into the space beyond the third circle and then be fed into that circle as well.

☆ Once you have finished, the third circle will probably be packed with exciting things to do. It takes a lot of time and effort to bring a calendar like this into full working order in your life, and it may be several years before everything finally slots into place. For now, highlight perhaps four or eight main celebrations that you would like to mark in the next year using a bright pen. The same pen might pick out a few personal celebrations that may be marked individually or with the support of the community (there may yet be lots of people who will dance on Toadspawn day!).

☆ About a month before a celebration is due, sit down and start planning the next celebration of people, spirit and Land. These might be both community-centred and myth-inspired (Christmas, for example, is both social and mythic – lots of family gatherings and the birth of a saviour). As a shaman exploring ways of bringing people and Land together, look for the environmental connection as well: Christmas coincides with the Midwinter Solstice, myth adds holly, ivy, oak and mistletoe, other traditions yield mumming plays and wassailing and it is a wonderful time to get people out of doors enjoying the seasons. Midwinter picnics in the frost are to be recommended. You will almost certainly find that your spirit family will have their own ideas to add as well and if you are working with the gods they will probably bring something else again.

9

Bringing It All
Back Home

The final test of a new shaman, of any shaman at any time, is their ability to anchor their work in the everyday lives of their people. Shamanism is one of the tools in a community's survival kit and as such must offer responses that are relevant, meaningful and can be acted upon. The shaman has to be able to bring whatever she learns in the spirit world back to her community in ways that the people can work with.

The Ceremonial Process

Different societies have their own ways of delivering and acting upon such information. The process is often a ceremonial one, a more or less formalised pattern of activity that allows the shaman to travel to the spirit world, do her work there, return, and convey her new understanding to her people. Such a ceremony might be a quiet one-to-one session with a patient or a full-scale song, drum and dance spectacle with a number of shamans in full panoply and the whole community gathered round.

All cultures have their own distinctive ceremonies that often identify their particular form of shamanism to outsiders: spirit canoes, spirit flight, Midewiwin false faces and Nyau spirit dancers to name a few. These forms have evolved (and go on evolving) with the relationships between those people, the land they live on and the spirits they work with. Sometimes those ceremonies migrate from one society to another, with neighbouring groups slowly adopting and adapting each other's ceremonies. The current trend for 'workshop shamanism', however, raises many questions, as ceremonies are taken and taught to 'outsiders' far from the land, people and spirits that gave them shape. Some of the shamans involved in this work have been told to do this by their spirits or their elders, while others may be motivated by a desire for a bit of quick cash, while tribal leaders and other shamans have objected to the whole situation, describing it as yet another form of colonial exploitation and claiming that ceremonies belong on the land or with the people that shaped them.

The modern shaman, starting with a blank page in her book of ceremonies, must try to decide what to do. She may see the needs of her people, hear the words of the spirits and see ways in which she could act, but she might not yet have ceremonies to work with. If she is working with a traditional system, that teaching should incorporate ceremonies as ways of involving her community in her work and she will have faced, or be facing, her own decisions about the use of such traditional material. She does have other options. Like a child with a set of building bricks, she might choose to make a house that takes elements from several different houses, or she might build a new house where perhaps other people could identify bits and pieces but where the overall building is new and remarkable and really fits into the landscape she is working in.

Most public shamanic work is ceremonial to some degree

in the sense that it has a structure, a framework that allows the shaman to do her work while her people can follow what is happening. There will be a distinct beginning, middle and end. People might be there as patients, observers or as active participants, and even a private consultation with a single patient can benefit from a ceremonial structure.

Bigger public ceremonies are often especially showy; dramatic events full of excitement and even sleight of hand trickery. A sceptical observer might see the whole thing as a sort of confidence trick and conclude that the whole ritual is a sham. But public ceremony is about performance. The performer, be she shaman, actor or priest, has to engage and hold the attention of her audience and find a way of drawing them into the action. How she chooses to do that is determined by the ceremonies of her culture and does not necessarily detract from her skills as a shaman. We may go to the cinema and watch a film knowing that it is all special effects and that no-one is really killed, but we still respond to the story being told, still relate to the characters, react to their situations and our emotions are drawn into what we see. This is the response a shaman is looking for in a public ceremony. The response to her work, the emotional commitment to what she is doing, feeds the shaman. She is acting on behalf of her people and their support of that action sustains her. It might look like glamour and deceit, but the shaman who cannot actually deliver the goods, who cannot bring back meaningful and useful responses to her people, is unlikely to hang on to that power for long.

Ceremonial Structure

In planning ceremonies there are a number of stages a new shaman needs to consider. The patterns described below are only one possible route to take but they provide a flexible framework upon which a shaman can build. The structures described might also be found in traditional ceremonies and when applied there can help a shaman understand the techniques used to achieve the various intentions of different stages in a ceremony.

The shaman can start by asking herself some questions:

☆ Why am I doing this? What are the everyday and the Otherworld reasons for this ceremony?

☆ What am I going to do? Has she already decided, or does she have a strong feeling about what techniques would be appropriate?

☆ When am I going to do it? Is this ceremony part of a calendar cycle, is it a response to an immediate need or is there a longer run-in time for a wedding or a naming ceremony perhaps? Does it feel that it needs woodland or open fields, night-time, a full moon or sunrise? The first frosts of winter or early spring sunshine?

Answering these questions will provide some picture of what might happen. With that information and any lively ideas for activity within the ceremony that she or her community or spirit family have come up with, she can start to build a structure. The whole thing might be seen as a series of stages:

☆ **Openings:** how do we arrive at our working space, how do we mark it as our own? Think about processions, spaces delineated by people, flags, lanterns, the walls of a building.

☆ **Welcome:** to all the participants. Who else should be invited or acknowledged? Prayers and offerings to ancestors, spirits of place, group totems, spirits of the four elements?

☆ **Intention:** remind everyone of what we are going to do and why.

☆ **Activity:** plan a number of actions that will involve some or all of the participants, as appropriate. Opportunities for contributions include dancing, singing and making music. Generate excitement: is the shaman entering trance now? Does someone else need to take over as Master of Ceremonies?

☆ **Climax:** the shaman in trance, the company all engaged as planned. Is the singing making the forest ring? Or is there silence with just the stamping feet, the breathing and the bells of a dancing shaman?

☆ **Relaxation:** the shaman returns and speaks. The company relaxes. Perhaps food is shared. This anchors the shaman in the everyday world and brings everyone together in a comfortable familiar activity.

☆ **Release:** the ceremony ends, perhaps with a reversal of the opening? Visitors are thanked, prayers offered, lanterns blown out. A procession home?

A shaman might find that she is already planning along lines like these, and with more experience these stages should flow smoothly into one another. With long-established ceremonies, the separate stages can often still be identified, but sometimes communities are so familiar with the language of their ceremonies that a simple action can imply a whole set of stages: a procession of horsemen gathering in a circle marks opening and intention, a raised feather fan signals a welcome.

A ceremony does not need to be loud and dramatic. Just as 'tools' were separated from 'techniques' back in Chapter 3, when planning a ceremony the shaman needs to separate intention – what each stage of a ceremony should achieve; action – how this is done; and atmosphere – the overall feeling. We tend to plan a ceremony with an overall intention followed by actions that feel relevant, however, the intention can get lost in the excitement of wanting to work with masks or a new drum or the chance to try some other technique. In an effective ceremony, the overall intention and the intent within any one stage are the most important things to consider. Build a ceremony as a pattern, weaving intention, action and atmosphere together with your understanding of people and place to create an event that will draw everyone into a powerful collective intention and action. Plan for your people as much as for yourself, finding actions and atmospheres that will help them realise the intent rather than choosing things just because you want to have a go with them. Listen to the spirits and do not forget their role in the proceedings or lose the heart of a ceremony in the precise stage-management of your planning.

For modern shamans, personal healing sessions or other work with individuals or small groups of people might easily follow traditional patterns, but where shamans are working with large groups of people other issues arise. Public trance work is seldom seen and rarely valued in our world. Indeed, communal celebrations of people and place have been rather scarce in this world for some time, but they are growing again now, providing a good chance for shamans to help people explore their relationship with the land. The shaman might find herself planning for several occasions: creating exciting dramatic public ceremonies for her people while conducting separate private trance sessions with the spirits and allowing the one to inform the other. It can make for a strange time for the shaman, finding ways of bridging new distances between the worlds, but it does work: the spirits still speak, inspire, guide and laugh, and in their celebrations, the shaman's people also tell stories, create dances, inspire and laugh.

Trance, Vision and other techniques allow the shaman to move between the worlds and speak to the spirits, but the measure of the shaman really lies in how she can bring that knowledge back to her people. A shaman belongs to her people, her work comes from the communities, both human and spirit, that she serves. They give her the power to act, the authority to speak on their behalf and she is answerable to them. They have the right to participate in the shaman's work and the variety of ceremonies allow them to do that. A ceremony might be big, dramatic and complicated but a simple conversation between a patient, a shaman and the spirits is just as much a ceremony. A shaman working outside of trance, leading a wedding, or a child's naming or opening a garden is still conducting a ceremony, helping her people explore and develop the relationships within themselves, within the community and with the land they live upon. In the end a shaman is measured by her deeds and is identified as a shaman not by herself but by the people she serves.

Rather than including a set of practical exercises in this chapter, there follow descriptions of two ceremonies, one a small personal healing event, the other a larger community celebration.

A Healing

☆ The drum is beating, a steady, hollow sound, and the scent of holy sage still hangs around the room. The shaman is kneeling beside her patient, who lies face down on the floor. The shaman sings softly to her spirits.

☆ The shaman passes her rattle along the length of her patient, holding it and shaking it vigorously a couple of hand-breadths above her back. The rattle sound cascades lightly, like snowflakes, down on to the patient's aura so the shaman can see it shining. The light identifies movement within the energy shell, patterns and tides, the ebb and flow of natural rhythms, and the problem areas, knots, interruptions and breaks.

☆ Her spirits are crowding round now, watching, sniffing, reaching out and touching the patient, releasing a knot here, a constriction there. And there! There! Dropping her rattle, the shaman plunges her hands into the mass of light, reaching down through aura and flesh to grasp and hold. The drumming is horse-gallop fast as she leans forward and sucks deeply. She turns and spits, almost vomiting, into a bowl of salt water by her side.

☆ The action is repeated twice over before the stain she has seen is gone. She has drained away as much as she can. It might return like an infection not yet conquered and a further extraction will be needed, but for now she and her spirits can work again on the energy flows, the rivers of light, and help the patient start her own healing process. The drumming slows, a gentle rhythm. It stops and a final rattling closes the session.

☆ While the drummer gives the tainted water to the earth so that the energy can be absorbed and used again in more creative ways, patient and shaman talk through the process, exchanging impressions and experiences. The drummer's role has been to support, not to diagnose or counsel, and now he brings in food and drink, then withdraws to allow privacy.

Hunting the Wren

'Hunting the Wren' is an old ceremony found in some of the Celtic countries. It takes place over the 12 days of Christmas, usually on 26 December, St Stephen's Day. In its traditional form, a group of boys kill a wren, parading its body through the village on a litter. Just why the wren is hunted is not clear: it might signify the change from the reign of the holly/wren king to the summer oak/robin king. In some cases, the wren seems to be a scapegoat, a repository for the ill-luck of the previous year, making sure it is not carried forward into the next.

The scapegoat theme was picked up in the creation of this new form of the ceremony.

☆ Fifty or so people gather round a fire at Midwinter. There is soup and hot bread, wine is mulling and the air is frosty. Away through the trees, a drum and penny whistle start up a hesitant little tune. The company falls quiet as a procession weaves through the trees, singing the hunting song:

> *How will you shoot her? said Milder to Molder,*
> *With bows and with arrows, said Fester to Foes.*
> *That will not do, said Milder to Molder*
> *What will do then? said Fester to Foes*
> *Guns and big cannons! says Johnny Rednose*

☆ As the procession enters, we can see four of their number carrying a litter at shoulder height. In the centre of it stands a little cage, woven from willow and thorn. The procession circles the fire, shepherding the rest of the company away from the flames to form a ring at the edge of the light. Putting aside food and drink, the company clap and stamp in time to the tune.

☆ The song ends and members of the procession pass through the company handing out small strips of cotton and pens. On one side of the cloth, visitors write what they would wish to be free of from the year that has gone and on the other the qualities they would invite into themselves for the year to come. Visitors approach the wren cage and slip their rags in through gaps in the woven twigs.

☆ The cage is full and the singing begins again, livelier now with everyone joining in on Johnny Rednose's increasingly outrageous and improvised responses. The parade starts with the whole company circling the fire, clapping, singing and drowning out the whistle and drum. At a signal from Top Hat, the leader of the troupe, everything stops and silently, reverently, the litter bearers approach the fire and lay the litter on it.

☆ In the quiet that follows, one singer sings 'Down in yon forest' and the gentle words carry across the chilly air. The fire takes the litter, the cage, the rags, releasing what we would be free of and sending the prayers of what we would become up with the sparks and out into the world.

> *Down in yon forest*
> *There stands a hall,*

The bells of paradise
I heard them ring.
It's covered all over with purple and gold
And I love the Old Forest above anything

☆ The ceremony ends in silence, but by then the mulling is ready and toasts are drunk, a wassail is sung and poured for the world, the spirits and the wild wrens that we cherish and will not hunt. Now the revelry can begin in earnest.

10

Passion and Obligation

Obligation

So now you stand here; Vision has inspired you, the spirits walk beside you and the gods have stamped on your head a few times.

Any shaman, apprentice, new or experienced, recognises the huge amounts he always has to learn. Even though we often work alone, a shaman should never be ashamed of learning from others, or asking others to help. As a patterner, I tend to refer people who are looking for healing on to someone else, while that shaman points groups looking for big ceremonies in my direction. Healers, in particular, need to practise their crafts under guidance. Lots of exciting terms are currently used in reference to healing: 'balancing the shields', 'soul-retrieval', 'spirit-catching', 'extraction' and more, but a shaman must be honest enough to admit, 'I haven't a clue' and go and find some training, or to say, 'No, this person actually needs to go to a doctor,' or 'All he really needs is someone to talk to, not a soul-retrieval and head-standing trance.'

And so it begins. Find people to talk to, to share experiences with, to relax and have a good laugh with. And so it will begin. It never ends. A shaman never stops learning. Shamans live in a world that changes all the time. Nothing is fixed, nothing can be taken for granted as the Web is always moving on. The shaman's path along the inward spiral will never end, even after he has stood in the centre of it all, for he will go on growing, learning and having new experiences. And the outward spiral will keep carrying him out into the world. Constancy, where it is found, lies, perhaps surprisingly, in the depths of the Otherworld. The Dreaming Land is often the thing that changes least. The Otherworld changes with the thoughts of people and spirits, the physical world reinvents itself constantly, but the hills go on slowly unfolding the shapes of the world, and the oldest spirits, the ancestors, the gods themselves, rest in those deepest layers of the spirit worlds. Everything else changes, a flowing, growing, unfolding change: a bud that flowers, dies, seeds itself and starts again. The Dream of the Land lasts.

A shaman belongs to his people, be they human or non-human, with bodies of flesh or only of spirit. His personal path may bring him a measure of power, the ability to work magic or to effect changes in the lives of those around him, but the authority to act is given by the people, by the spirits, by the gods. And there the shaman's obligation lies: to serve those who come to him. Service, of course, is a twisted path and the trickster's deceit or the barbed comments of a healer can throw the enquirer into confusion. Unfortunately, while a shaman is there to serve, he is not necessarily there to be nice to anyone, and sometimes the most effective healers are those who scare the wits out of their patients. His integrity lies within his Vision and the honesty of his heart; he is true to the Web and the patterns of connection that spin out across the world, and his community must have confidence in that sense of honour. They may not understand it but they know that he acts out of his own depth of integrity and compassion. A shaman is fierce or tricky or gentle because he sees a way in that for his people to find their own paths through life, not because he is bitter or vindictive.

Passion

Finally, there is passion. Throughout this book passion has run below the surface, showing a fin here and there but rarely breaking the waves of principle and obligation. It is difficult to describe a shaman's passion. In part it is filled with small things – the beauty of pigeons bathing in a puddle, the trilling roar and shoal-like flight of starlings coming in to roost, the trees, a spider, the smell of food. It is endless. Passion opens the heart and becomes a compassion that reaches out, smiling at the world, ready to slap it or hug it as need be. Sometimes we are tired and grumpy, sometimes we wish the world would leave us alone, but then we watch the candle flame, laugh at silliness, and reconnect.

Passion is also in big things. Passion lies in a glory that burns like a sunset over the sea, in the blood of being hunted through the woods of the Otherworld and the wonder of being stone. Passion lies in the gods who take us apart, who love us and put us back together again, in a dance that never ends, that fills the heart and spirit, that moves and burns everything else away. Passion lies in spirits soaring in the empty spaces between the worlds. Passion hides itself inside us. It keeps us going.

A Final Reminder

I live no life,
But the life the earth gives me

I breathe no breath,
but of the air the earth sends me.

I live every moment,
The Goddess grants me.

Useful Addresses

UK

Eagles' Wing, 58 Westbere Road, London, NW2 3RU.
  Website: www.shamanism.co.uk
The Raven Lodge, 35 Wilson Avenue, Deal, Kent, CT14 9NL.
  E-mail: information@ravenlodge.prestel.co.uk
Centre for Shamanic Studies, 29 Chambers Lane, London,
  NW10 2JR.
The Sacred Trust, PO Box 603, Bath BA1 2ZU

EUROPE

Scandinavian Centre for Shamanic Studies, Jonathon Horwitz
  and Annette Høst, Artillerivej 63, LEJL. 140, DK-2300,
  Copenhagen, S Denmark

USA

Foundation for Shamanic Studies, PO Box 1939, Mill Valley,
  California 94942, USA. Website: www.shamanism.org

MAGAZINES AND JOURNALS

These are often the easiest way of finding out what is happening – current workshops and where to get equipment.

Shaman's Drum, PO Box 97, Ashland, OR 97520, USA. E-mail: sdrm@mind.net

(A journal of experential shamanism.)

Sacred Hoop, PO Box 16, Narberth, Pembrokeshire, SA67 8YG, UK. Website: www.sacredhoop.demon.uk

(A practical guide to living with spirit.)

Spirit Talk, 120 Argyle Street, Cambridge, CB1 3LS.

Further Reading

Alford, V., *The Hobby Horse and Other Animal Masks*, Merlin Press, 1978

Bates, B., *The Way of Wyrd*, HarperCollins, 1992

Bates, B., *The Wisdom of the Wyrd*, Rider, 1996

Baggot, A., *Celtic Wisdom; A Piatkus Guide*, Piatkus, 1999

Bloom, W., *Working With Angels, Fairies and Nature Spirits*, Piatkus, 1998

Breeden, S. and Wright, B., *Kakadu*, Simon & Schuster, 1989

Briggs, K., *A Dictionary of Fairies*, Allen Lane, 1976 (reprinted, Pantheon, 1998)

Brown, J.E., *Animals of the Soul*, Element, 1992

Brown, J.E., *The Sacred Pipe*, University of Oklahoma, 1953

Cahill, S. and Halpern, J., *The Ceremonial Circle*, Mandala, 1991

Campbell, J., *Historical Atlas of World Mythology, Vol. 1: The Way of the Animal Powers*, Harper & Row, 1988

Connor, R.P., *Blossom of Bone*, HarperCollins, 1993

Fire, J. and Erdoes, R., *Lame Deer: Sioux Medicine Man*, Davis-Poynter Ltd, 1973

Foster, S. and Little, M., *Vision Quest*, Simon & Schuster, 1992

Fries, J., *Visual Magic*, Mandrake, 1992

Froud, B. and Lee, A., *Faeries*, Pan Books, 1979

Goodman, F.J., *Where the Spirits Ride the Wind*, Indiana University Press, 1990

Gordon the Toad, *Small Acts of Magic*, Creeping Toad, 1994

Halifax, J., *Shaman: The Wounded Healer*, Thames & Hudson, 1982

Halifax, J., *Shamanic Voices*, Penguin, 1991

Harner, M., *The Way of the Shaman*, Harper & Row, 1980

Harvey, G. and Hardman, C., *Paganism Today*, Thorsons, 1996

Heth, C. (ed.), *Native American Dance*, Fulcrum/Smithsonian, 1992

Hole, C., *A Dictionary of British Folk Customs*, Paladin Books, 1978

Hunt, W.B., *The Complete How-To Book of Indiancraft*, Collier Macmillan, 1973

Jackson, A. *Instruments Around the World*, Longman, 1988

Jamal, M., *Deerdancer*, Arkana, 1995

Lawlor, R., *Voices of the First Day*, Inner Traditions International, 1991

MacLellan, G., *Sacred Animals*, Capall Bann, 1997

MacLellan, G., *Talking to the Earth*, Capall Bann, 1995

Minor, M. and N., *The American Indian Craft Book*, University of Nebraska, 1978

Neihardt, J.G. (DeMallie, R., ed.), *The Sixth Grandfather*, Bison Books, 1985

Rockwell, D., *Giving Voice to Bear*, Roberts Rinehart, 1991

Roden, S., *Sound Healing*, Piatkus, 1999

Seed, J., *Thinking Like a Mountain*, Heretic Books, 1988

Starhawk, *Dreaming the Dark*, Beacon Press, 1982

Van der Post, L., *The Heart of the Hunter*, Penguin, 1965

Vitebsky, P., *The Shaman*, Macmillan, 1995

Wall, S., *Wisdom's Daughters*, HarperPerennial, 1994

Wall, S. and Arden, H., *Wisdomkeepers*, Beyond World Publishing, 1990

Willis, R., (ed.), *World Mythology*, Piatkus, 1997

Index

Piatkus Guides, written by experts, combine background information with practical exercises, and are designed to change the way you live.
Titles include:

Tarot Cassandra Eason

Tarot's carefully graded advice enables readers to obtain excellent readings from Day One. You will quickly gain a thorough knowledge of both Major and Minor Arcanas and their symbolism, and learn how to use a variety of Tarot spreads.

Meditation Bill Anderton

Meditation covers the origins, theory and benefits of meditation. It includes over 30 meditations and provides all the advice you need to mediate successfully.

Crystal Wisdom Andy Baggott and Sally Morningstar

Crystal Wisdom is a fascinating guide to the healing power of crystals. It details the history and most popular modern uses of crystals and vibrational healing. It also covers colour, sound and chakra healing, and gem, crystal and flower essences.

Celtic Wisdom Andy Baggott

Celtic Wisdom is a dynamic introduction to this popular subject. The author covers Celtic spirituality, the wisdom of trees, animals and stones, ritual and ceremony and much more.

Feng Shui Jon Sandifer

Feng Shui introduces the origins, theory and practice of the Chinese art of perfect placement, or geomancy. It provides easy-to-follow techniques to help you carry out your own readings and create an auspicious living space.

The Essential Nostradamus Peter Lemesurier

The Essential Nostradamus charts the life of this extraordinary man, and includes newly discovered facts about his life and work. Peter Lemesurier unravels his prophecies for the coming decades.

New titles

Psychic Awareness   Cassandra Eason

Psychic Awareness is a fascinating guide to using the power of your mind to enhance your life. Simple exercises will develop your abilities in clairvoyance, telepathy, detecting ghosts, dowsing and communicating with a spirit guide.

Reiki   Penelope Quest

Reiki explains the background to this healing art and how it can improve your physical health and encourage personal and spiritual awareness and growth. Discover how simple Reiki is to use, whether for self-healing or treating other people.

Kabbalah   Paul Roland

Kabbalah is an accessible guide to the origins, principles and beliefs of this mystical tradition. It includes original meditations and visualisations to help you gain higher awareness and understanding.

Colour Healing   Pauline Wills

Colour Healing explains the vital role colour plays in your physical, emotional and spiritual well-being and how it is used in healing. Meditations and practical exercises will help you to discover the vibrational energies of all the colours of the rainbow.

Tibetan Buddhism   Stephen Hodge

Tibetan Buddhism explains the basic teachings and central concepts of Tibetan Buddhism. There is also guidance on basic meditation, the nature of offerings and worship, and the requirements for embarking on Tantric practice.

Maya Prophecy   Dr Ronald Bonewitz

Maya Prophecy is an intriguing introducting to the prophetic warnings for the future from one of the greatest early civilisations. It explores how Maya religion, mathematics and the Maya calendar provide support for the veracity of the prophecy, and how you should prepare for what lies ahead.

New titles

Angels   Paul Rowland

Angels shows you the purpose and hierarchy of angels and how to contact them and experience their love and advice. Find out how our Guardian Angels protect us and how to ask for guidance and inspiration.

Shamanism   Gordon MacLellan

Shamanism is a helpful introduction to the key concepts of shamanism and how to use them in your life. Learn how these ancient powers for healing and creativity can be used in many modern situations

Forthcoming November 1999:

Earth mysteries   Paul Devereux

Earth Mysteries is an authoritative and easy-to-read analysis of the mysteries surrounding ancient sacred sites. It includes information on mysterious energies, sacred geometry and ley lines.

Astrology   Carole Golder

Astrology is a fascinating introduction to the principles of astrology with new insights into working with the positive and negative aspects of your sign

Pendulum Dowsing   Cassandran Eason

Pendulum Dowsing is an accessible exploration of the history of dowsing and the techniques used to find lost objects, channel healing forces and tune into the psychic world.

Forthcoming January 2000

Druidry   Philip Shallcross

Learn the history and development of druidry, its divination methods and healing traditions. Discover how understanding the ancient wisdom of the druids can help unlock your creativity and inspiration

Native American Wisdom   Grey Wolf

A fascinating insight into Native American culture and the traditional ceremonies and tools used for spiritual healing. Discover the essential bond between ourselves and the spirit world.